"I am honoured to provide a strong recommendation to read Canon Andrew White's extraordinary book. I came to know and respect Canon White when we worked in Iraq in the hectic days following Saddam's overthrow. I now serve on the Board of his not-for-profit organization which helps refugees and the underprivileged in the Middle East. This well-written book is full of Andrew's light humour and deep Christian faith. We learn of the rich spiritual life of his parents and then are taken on the wonderful voyage of Andrew's own spiritual growth over the next forty years. Andrew's lifelong struggle with health problems has only increased his devotion and faith. The book is a fitting tribute to his lifelong faith and continued work for the poor and the forgotten."

Ambassador Paul Bremer, former Presidential Envoy to Iraq

"Andrew White is the most extraordinary friend I have. His story so far is a rollercoaster of a journey – and this is not fiction! This story will infuse faith, hope and love."

Revd Canon J.John

"Abouna Andrew is for us in Iraq not just a spiritual leader for the Christians: he is the spiritual leader of all of us – Iraqis, Sunni, Shia, and others. He has stood with us and been our supporter and defender for nearly two decades. When people were too afraid even to come to Iraq he stayed with us. He is like the Almighty: he will never leave us. However hard the circumstances he is with us."

Grand Ayatollah Hussein Al-Sadr, The Grand Ayatollah of Khadameer, Baghdad

"Canon Andrew White has devoted his life to the true mission of religion – to assist, comfort and save lives of human beings in the most difficult places of conflict. He is a messenger of divine peace in the world, and a great friend of the Jewish people."

Rabbi Melchior, Chief Rabbi of Norway, and former Member of the Knesset

ANDREW WHITE
My JOURNEY SO FAR

LION

Published by Lion Books
an imprint of
Lion Hudson plc
Wilkinson House, Jordan Hill Road,
Oxford OX2 8DR, England
www.lionhudson.com/lion

ISBN 978 0 7459 7022 6
e-ISBN 978 0 7459 7018 9

First edition 2015

Acknowledgments
Plate section pictures supplied by and reproduced with kind permission of FRRME

Extract pp. 52–54 taken from 'Charles Simeon: Pastor of a Generation' by Handley Moule, published by Christian Focus Publications, Fearn, Ross-shire, Scotland www.christianfocus.com

Extract p. 221 taken from *All Of Us* by Raymond Carver, copyright © 1997 Raymond Carver. Published by Harvill Press. Reprinted by permission of The Random House Group Limited and The Wylie Agency.

Scripture quotations marked "NIV" are taken from the Holy Bible, New International Version Anglicised Copyright © 1979, 1984, 2011 Biblica, formerly International Bible Society. Used by permission of Hodder & Stoughton Ltd, an Hachette UK company. All rights reserved. "NIV" is a registered trademark of Biblica UK trademark number 1448790.

Other Scripture versions used:
Scripture quotations marked "NKJV" are taken from the New King James Version®. Copyright © 1982 by Thomas Nelson. Used by permission. All rights reserved.

Scripture quotations marked "KJV" are taken from The Authorized (King James) Version. Rights in the Authorized Version in the United Kingdom are vested in the Crown. Reproduced by permission of the Crown's patentee, Cambridge University Press.

A catalogue record for this book is available from the British Library

Printed and bound in the UK, October 2015, LH26

*I dedicate this book
to my mother,
Pauline S. White*

Contents

Acknowledgments 9

Foreword by The Rt Revd Dr Michael Nazir-Ali 11

Chapter 1 An Unusual Beginning 13

Chapter 2 Turbulence 23

Chapter 3 Just Like Heaven 35

Chapter 4 Called by God 45

Chapter 5 The Academic Hothouse 51

Chapter 6 A Prophetic Word 61

Chapter 7 Life-defining Events 69

Chapter 8 A New Life 79

Chapter 9 Several Landmarks 87

Chapter 10 Sent to Coventry 95

Chapter 11 To the Middle East 105

Chapter 12 Return to Iraq 113

Chapter 13 The Road to Alexandria 123

Chapter 14 Relief and Reconciliation Go Hand in Hand 131

Chapter 15 Back to Coventry 141

Chapter 16 Brought Back to Life 153

Chapter 17	An Oasis of Healing	161
Chapter 18	Don't Take Care; Take Risks	169
Chapter 19	A Normal Day	181
Chapter 20	The Bigger Picture	189
Chapter 21	My Choice	197
Chapter 22	Very Special People	203
Afterword	Tariq Aziz	215
Epilogue	Late Fragment	217

Acknowledgments

Whenever I attempt to thank all the people who deserve to be acknowledged, who have helped in the writing of one of my books, there are always far too many – but I want, at least, to list the bare minimum.

I have to mention my family. First of all, the people who have put up with me the longest: my wonderful mother, Pauline White, my wonderful wife, Caroline, and my dear sons, Josiah and Jacob.

In addition to my children are my godchildren and especially those closest to me: Alexander Muir, Hannah-Rivkah Martin-Thomas, and Alice Cross. I thank God for these people every day – each is an inspiration in my life.

Thank you to all my staff in the UK, Israel, Iraq, Jordan, and the US. Special thanks go to Lesley Kent and Phillip Rowdan, my assistants in the UK, and Hanna Ishaq, my assistant in Israel.

I also acknowledge those who have been closest to me in Baghdad: my unofficial adopted children, Dawood, his wife, Sandy, and their baby, Andrew, dear Fulla, who now lives in Chicago, and Sally Multi, who is still in Baghdad.

One other person I must mention is Dr Sarah Ahmed, who essentially runs my life.

Finally, I cannot thank enough those who made this book possible: my publisher, Tony Collins, and his team at Lion Hudson, and my wonderful editor, Tim Pettingale. Thank you so much. You are all the greatest.

Foreword

I have known Andrew for a long time, especially as his mother lived in my former diocese of Rochester. It was, however, not until he asked me to visit him in Baghdad that I began to realise what a remarkable person he is. In this book he mentions the need religious leaders have for comfortable accommodation at conferences. This is certainly not the case with him! He lived, as he says, in the simplest possible way in one room in a small house next to St George's Church. I have stayed with him there and I do not know how he managed it, particularly with his debilitating illness.

Andrew has a talent for being in the wrong place at the wrong time – at least from a human point of view! Whether it is the intifada in Israel/Palestine or terrorism in Baghdad, there he is! This may be frustrating for security-wallahs, diplomats, and policy makers but for Andrew it is because of his obedience to divine direction.

His ministry at St George's has been nothing short of miraculous and we must pray that it will continue with the most remarkable Iraqi Christians there, now that Andrew no longer is. It has been, and is, an example of holistic mission with worship, prayer, healing (medical and spiritual), feeding, witnessing, and loving all going on side by side.

Andrew has been driven by his own Isaiah Vision, drawn from Isaiah 61:1–4. This has led him to love the unlovely, to befriend the friendless, to bring enemies face to face so they can become friends and to hold together reconciliation and relief for the hungry, the homeless, and the sick. The results are there for all to see.

Although the world has seen him, most recently, as the "Vicar of Baghdad", in fact his vision is for the whole of the Middle East. It may be that he is being led back to addressing the wider task of reconciliation and peace in that violent part of the world.

It is not just Andrew's work, of course, that deserves notice, but the miracle of his personal story. The immediacy of his walk and his talk with his God is obvious to anyone who is with him for any length of time. He is himself the "wounded healer" bringing healing to others, whilst being seriously ill himself. In this, he is a witness to the crucified Christ, the One he serves with heart, mind, and body. We need also to note the sacrifices made by his family in releasing him for this ministry. Let us hope that they will now see a little more of him.

I am glad he has written this book so that we can better understand his passionate commitments and his strong faith in the One who continues to sustain him.

The Rt Revd Dr Michael Nazir-Ali,
former Bishop of Rochester

CHAPTER 1

An Unusual Beginning

My earliest memory is of being told how much Jesus loved me. I was brought up in a Christian household and my parents took every opportunity to reveal the love of God to me. Consequently, I cannot remember a time when I didn't know about Jesus: He was part of my life right from the beginning, and I loved Him just as much as He loved me.

Even without being told, I guessed that I should speak to Jesus every day, so I did. My parents would pray with me every night while settling me into bed, and then I knew that it was my time to talk with Him. My childlike prayer ran the same way each night:

Dear Lord Jesus, I love you so much. Thank you for loving me so much too. Thank you for hearing and answering my prayers.

To this day, I begin my night-time prayers with these same words. Until now I have never written them down, and doing so makes me feel like bursting into tears. I'm trying hard to avoid doing this, however, since I'm writing on an aeroplane!

I can't have been much older than two when I began praying that prayer – essentially, as soon as I could talk – but this is how real Jesus has been to me for my entire life. I hope this will explain why I cannot recall a single moment when I had what most people call a "conversion experience". I had always loved Jesus and I knew in my heart that He loved me, so there was no "before and after" Jesus for me; there was just Jesus, ever present.

I have, however, never doubted the reality of my salvation. Even when I was studying theology at Cambridge, and was surrounded by a great number of doubting people, my faith was secure.

When I speak in churches, I like to tease the congregation by telling them that I have never been converted. People tend to react with a mixture of disbelief, shock, and horror!

Our household was a Christian one, but not Anglican. My father, Maurice White, was a staunch Calvinist, and my mother, Pauline, came from a classical Assemblies of God Pentecostal background. As a result, my faith was formed in a melting pot of church cultures. The act of coming to faith in the Pentecostal Church stream tends to emphasize "giving one's heart to Christ". There are lots of altar calls in Pentecostal churches, which focus on encouraging people to "make a decision to follow Jesus". As a child, I was slightly concerned for a while that I had never officially "given my heart to Jesus" and I wasn't entirely sure what it meant. In my childlike way, I tried to work out how one might do this, so I literally cut a heart shape out of paper in order somehow to give it to Him!

A contented childhood

I have only wonderful memories of the vast majority of my childhood, and I was an exceptionally happy child. With me were my sister, Joanna, two years older than me, and Mark, my younger brother by just eleven months. We were not a wealthy household – in fact, quite a poor one – but we were very content. Though poor, one thing we didn't lack were toys, of which there was an abundance because most of them were made by my father.

My father was of Anglo-Indian descent, coming from a somewhat strange tribe of British Indians who were a product of the Raj. He had grown up in a very distinguished, influential family, but had chosen to marry my mother, much to his family's disapproval. His parents didn't view her as having the "right" social background, since she came from humble, working-class stock. In due course my father was disinherited and he and my mother ended up living a simple life in a poorer part of London.

Yet Mother had a rich spiritual heritage. Her father had studied at one of the first Assemblies of God Bible colleges in the UK and, after graduation, went to work alongside Smith Wigglesworth, one of the greatest Pentecostal leaders of all time. Today I am good friends with Henry Fardell, Wigglesworth's great-grandson, and the Pentecostal pioneer's influence continues to reverberate down the generations.

My father was an exceptionally bright man. He had degrees in Biological Sciences, Civil Engineering, and Theology. He knew all the classical languages and could write fluently in both Latin and Classical Greek. But it was his grasp of mathematics that totally baffled me. He would try to teach me maths and I could never understand it. Of his three children, I was considered the one with the nicest personality, but not the brightest.

Of the many toys that my father made for us, two in particular were very important to me. The first was a little wooden farmyard. It had authentic wooden outbuildings surrounded by a cluster of wooden trees. I would populate my farm with an array of plastic farm animals and spend hours just moving them around, acting out what I thought farm life must be like. One thing that was slightly different about my farm was that my favourite animal was a kangaroo! I don't know why, but I had a fondness for kangaroos. I also had a soft one, knitted by my mother, complete with a baby roo in its pouch.

My other memorable toy came when I was older and lasted for several years. It was the most amazing wooden go-cart. It was constructed mainly from wood, but my father built it like a vintage Rolls-Royce, with a properly functioning steering wheel, highly effective suspension, and a metal "bonnet" fashioned after the house-shaped angles of the Silver Ghost. It was simply an amazing piece of work, and I cherished it.

My pseudo-Rolls go-cart had one other interesting feature: the bonnet could be lifted up to reveal a storage compartment. Inside this I kept an extensive first-aid kit. As with my ever-present faith, I have always had a fascination with medicine. It is hard to say when this began, but during my go-carting years first aid was a major interest of mine.

It was no surprise to anyone that, aged nine, I decided to join the St John Ambulance Brigade. St John had the wonderful foresight to provide training for young boys and girls, thereby ensuring their legacy would continue into the future.

Thursday evenings were Brigade meetings and the highlight of my week, when we would come together for first-aid lessons and to practise the techniques we had already been taught. As I look back, forty years on, I am amazed by just how much I was taught, despite the fact that I was a child. But, for me, being taught something wasn't enough; I wanted to practise! So I began treating all the children in my neighbourhood whenever they had minor accidents. I know it sounds strange now, but if I heard that anyone had been hurt, I would go in my go-cart to find them, get my first-aid kit out, and treat them. My go-cart was like an unofficial junior ambulance. Eventually even the local doctor heard about and complimented me on my first-aid skills!

SPIRITUAL FORMATION

The majority of my formative years were spent soaking up information like a sponge. While other boys were out playing football, I was on a steep learning curve, taking in equal measures of information about medicine and spirituality.

I remember that one of the first books that was ever read to me was Bunyan's *The Holy War*, which he wrote in 1682 while serving a twelve-year sentence in prison for preaching without a licence. Yes, my experiences were very different from those that most children had. I also recall being taught what were, in essence, complex theological concepts, so that by the age of six I could recite the five points of Calvinism with the acronym TULIP:

T*otal Depravity*
U*nconditional Election*

17

Limited Atonement
Irresistible Grace
Perseverance of the Saints

This I didn't just repeat parrot-fashion – I could actually say what each point meant.

Sundays were a mix of spiritual traditions. In the morning the whole family would attend a Strict Baptist Sunday school, followed by their morning service. Then we would rush home for our Sunday lunch, before heading to the large Assemblies of God church nearby for their afternoon Sunday school. We would take a packed tea with us and stay on for their evening service.

Just to add yet another dimension to my spiritual education, my father had an unusually philo-Semitic understanding of his faith, and therefore taught me not only about Christianity but also about Judaism. He showed me that Judaism was in fact the foundation of the Christian faith. I also became aware of the evils of anti-Semitism and learned about the Holocaust. Our family lived in an area of London that had traditionally been a Jewish neighbourhood and therefore had one of the largest Jewish cemeteries. As a young boy I took the issue of anti-Semitism very seriously, and though I had never seen the cemetery being attacked I was aware that it could be, so I would regularly go and stand outside its gates to "guard" it.

While other children were reading *The Beano* or *The Dandy*,[1] I spent my time reading about Judaism and medicine. By the age of ten my main reading material was *A Jewish*

---

1   *The Beano* is a British children's comic, published by D. C. Thomson & Co., which first appeared in 1938. *The Dandy* was published by the same company from 1937 to 2012.

Theology by Rabbi Louis Jacobs[2] and *An Introduction to Surgery.* Alongside these I would read many complementary works, spending hours in the local library searching out the right kind of books to take home and devour.

What do you want to be when you grow up?

I remember one day at school when our form teacher informed us that we all needed to consider what we wanted to do when we grew up. Many of my peers had no idea what they wanted to do, but I was always very clear about it, if rather unconventional. I was keen to pursue my twin passions of faith and medicine. I knew enough about the latter to have established a specific area of interest: anaesthetics. I wanted to be both a priest and an anaesthetist, and told my teacher so. I was told that I could do one or the other, but not both.

I had a similar conversation with my parents. This time I was told that I could go into medicine if I wanted to, but I couldn't be a "priest" since I was a Strict Baptist and they didn't have priests. None of this deterred me, though. I felt that God had put this twin calling on my life and that, somehow, Jesus was going to help me to do all that I was supposed to do in life.

Around this time I made an unlikely friend who was to have a profound effect on my spiritual formation and help put me on the path towards becoming a priest. Living on the same road as our family was an old lady who was bedridden. No one ever laid eyes on her, but we often heard about "Miss Davis", especially from her sister, who lived

---

2   Published by Behrman House Publishing, 1973.

right next door to us. One day I asked our neighbour if I would be allowed to go and see Miss Davis, her sister. I was assured that she would love to meet me and the same day I was invited round to her house.

Immediately we became firm friends, and from that day forward Miss Davis became "Aunty Hilda" to me. I visited her almost every day and discovered that she had a profoundly deep faith in and love for Jesus. We would pray together about all manner of things; she was a wonderful lady. There was just one problem: Aunty Hilda was not a Baptist, or even a Pentecostal; she was a member of the Church of England. Sad to say, in the Baptist/Pentecostal circles I moved in during the seventies, Anglicans were not even considered "real" Christians. Yet it was clear to me that here was a lady of authentic faith, who knew God and loved Him deeply.

Because Aunty Hilda was unable to leave her house owing to ill health, her local priest would visit every week to minister Holy Communion. This same priest visited our school each week. Before long he invited me to go and visit Aunty Hilda's church and I was most curious to see what it might be like, so I asked my parents' permission and arranged to go.

In due course I entered a different world – church as I had never experienced it before. It was smells and bells and high-church Anglo-Catholic liturgy. To me as a ten-year-old boy, it seemed like a glimpse into what I imagined heaven was like, and I immediately fell in love with it.

This meant that my churchgoing activities were about to become considerably more complicated, with my Sundays spent dashing from one place to the next. My morning would begin with the Anglicans at 7.00 a.m., followed by a rush to get to the Strict Baptist service and later the Assemblies of God service.

It was a clash of church cultures but I was drawn to the Anglican model of church and began attending more of Aunty Hilda's church's services. Each day after school, I would run out of the door in order to get to church in time for their Evensong service, which would be conducted according to the 1662 Book of Common Prayer. On Saturdays I would also attend their Communion service. After a while I was asked if I would be a server. I was delighted to do so and greatly enjoyed dressing up in a robe. I recall walking to the church with the priest one Sunday morning and mentioning to him all the services I would be attending that day. He said to me, "Andrew, don't you get indigestion with all this church?"

I admit it was strange, but I loved it.

CHAPTER 2

Turbulence

Having enjoyed a blissfully happy existence up to the end of my pre-teen years, I suddenly began to experience some personal health problems and, around the same time, some family turmoil.

I had suffered with minor ear and throat troubles for a few years, but these hadn't bothered me much to begin with. When I was eleven, however, they became a lot worse and persisted to the point where they were causing me chronic problems. It was decided that I needed both a tonsillectomy and a myringotomy, the latter to relieve pressure in my eardrum caused by the build-up of excess fluid, so I was admitted to hospital. Some children would have found this an ordeal, but to me it was an adventure.

My first experience of entering an operating theatre is indelibly printed on my mind. By now I was well read in the theory of anaesthetics and was very pleased to be meeting a real-life anaesthetist. It must have been strange for him, I'm sure, to have an eleven-year-old boy asking him why he was still using cyclopropane in his anaesthetic machine, and did he not consider it dangerous to do so? (At the time, questions were being asked about its safety and today cyclopropane is no longer used.) I remember him telling me that it was a very good induction agent for children because of its sweet smell. I had to agree, and thoroughly enjoyed the sensation of being anaesthetized!

The next sensation I became aware of was not so pleasant, however. I came round to find myself vomiting blood. It wasn't just a little, and the doctors bustled around me, clearly very worried. They set up a blood transfusion and I was admitted to a ward to recover. I had entered hospital early that morning and it was almost midnight by the time they were satisfied that it was safe for me to have my operation. I was taken back to theatre and saw the same consultant anaesthetist, still on duty. I managed to have another conversation with him and asked another unlikely question for a young boy: "Are you going to use cricoid pressure?" (an emergency procedure used whenever there is a risk of the stomach filling with blood). He assured me that he would, if it became necessary.

After the operation my recovery was slow, but as soon as I was feeling well enough to go out I was taken on one of my father's trips into central London. These were regular excursions and, whatever else happened, always featured certain events. Lunch would be taken in my father's favourite Indian restaurant, Anwar's in Gower Street, off the Tottenham Court Road. I loved this place. I first visited Anwar's at the age of four and I was very sad when it closed recently.

Another regular feature was a visit to Charing Cross Road to one of the many bookshops for which my father and I shared a passion. Our favourite was Foyles, the largest bookstore in Europe at that time. Downstairs, on the lower ground floor, was a huge medical department. On this trip I was allowed to select a book of my choice for having endured my surgery. I headed straight for the anaesthetics section and picked out *Lee's Synopsis of Anaesthesia*, still widely regarded as a comprehensive classic on the subject. Today, this volume has pride of place on the bookshelf of my study at home in England.

I suppose one could say that before I'd entered my teens, the foundation of my life was set: a love for the church, both Anglican and Pentecostal branches, a passion for medicine, particularly anaesthetics, and an interest in Judaism.

FAMILY TRIBULATIONS

After I recovered from surgery, life returned to normal for a while, but it was about to change radically. My dear sister, Joanna, was becoming increasingly ill and no one could find out exactly what was wrong with her. She had stopped eating and was clearly mentally distressed. She went from doctor to doctor, hospital to hospital, all to no avail. My parents took her to see private doctors in Harley Street, which evidently they couldn't afford, but it was a long time before any conclusions were reached.

Eventually, it was established that she was suffering from a mental illness, which manifested itself as anorexia nervosa. This was at a time when very little was known about the condition. Joanna spent hours crying and screaming and life became intolerable for her. This had a dramatic effect on the rest of the family and we all lived in fear of her extreme behaviour. She would often be taken into a psychiatric unit for long periods and, sad to say, these were the only times when it was bearable to be at home.

I found it very difficult to cope with Joanna's sickness. I remember walking home from school with my brother,

Mark, both of us praying that when we arrived Joanna would not be in her "crazy" state. Most of the time, however, she was. As a result, I spent more and more time with Aunty Hilda. Sadly, though, it wasn't long before Hilda was too frail to continue living on her own and she was taken into a Christian convent hospital on the other side of London. This caused me considerable pain and distress.

Time during the school holidays was spent out of the house as much as possible. A typical day would see Mark and me travelling by bus all over London on a "Red Rover" unlimited travel ticket, as we took in the capital's bookstores, libraries, and museums.

It soon became clear to us boys that my parents wanted to relocate out of the city, so that we could grow up in a better area, attend better schools, and perhaps provide Joanna with a more peaceful environment. They were thinking of moving to Kent, known as the Garden of England, and were interested in going to Bexley. I knew the area fairly well – it was where my maternal grandparents lived and where my mother had grown up.

At the grand old age of twelve I thought that I was mature enough to do the house hunting on behalf of the family, and this I did quite successfully. I found a good house in the right area, which my parents subsequently bought. It was much larger and far nicer than the one we'd been used to in London. We started attending excellent new schools and really appreciated the new area. But my sister continued to have serious health challenges and was constantly in and out of hospital. Her anorexia was so severe that at one point she weighed a mere four stone, and she was five foot two inches tall. So, in this regard, life remained difficult.

Church continued to play a major role in my life. We attended a local Strict Baptist chapel and also found a local Assemblies of God church. I found an Anglican church to attend, but it was nothing like the Anglo-Catholic one I had been a member of in London, and consequently I never joined it.

Around this time I made a close friend for the first time in my life. Brian Heath went to a local United Reformed church and attended the same school as me. We would often do our homework/prep together. The other thing we used to love doing was looking for frogs in a local stream. We gathered such an impressive collection of frogs that we had to create a pond especially for them in my back garden at home. We gave them all biblical names. I can remember Obadiah, Malachi and, from the New Testament, Bartholomew! The rest of my time was spent attending church meetings and visiting older people.

I became very friendly with one particular couple. Retired Colonel Watson was British, but had formerly served in the Indian Army Ordnance Corps. Like much of my family, Col and Mrs Watson were products of the British Raj, and lived in India until independence in 1947. At that time Col Watson had returned to England and spent the rest of his career in the British military as a Brigadier General. (It puzzled me that he was always referred to as "the Colonel", but I never did get to the bottom of it.) I would spend hours in conversation with both of them at the front gate of their house. Eventually the Colonel died and thereafter I became very close to Mrs Watson, who was a surrogate "Aunty Hilda" to me. I visited her regularly after school and often did my homework at her house. The other thing about going to Mrs Watson's bungalow was that she had a television – an item that was forbidden in our house while we remained of school age – so I became a secret TV watcher!

Serious illness

During my first summer vacation in Kent I realized that I wanted to do something to help other people in our community. I went to the local volunteer centre and they sent me to visit a place called the Pop-in Parlour, or PIP as it was known, a place where elderly people could meet, drink tea, and chat with one another.

I liked the PIP and immediately became wholeheartedly involved. It was normal to give about two hours of your time to serving there, but I tended to stay all day – not just chatting with the many diverse visitors, as was expected, but also cleaning the centre from top to bottom. I got to know the people who came along quite well and they told me about the various needs they had at home, so increasingly I began to visit their homes to help them. Life soon became centred on the PIP and this continued after the summer holidays. I would spend my Saturdays working there and I loved it. Then, a seemingly innocuous accident had a very dramatic effect on my life.

I travelled everywhere on my bike. One weekend, cycling home from the PIP, I hit a bump in the road and fell off, cutting my right knee quite badly on the gravel. Being St John-trained, I cleaned and dressed the wound myself, then took myself off to the local hospital. The A&E staff were quite concerned because there still seemed to be some gravel embedded deep within the wound. They cleaned and re-dressed the wound and I was sent home.

The wound did not heal properly, however, and soon became badly infected. The hospital doctors decided that I would need an operation, which in due course I had, but soon afterwards the wound broke down and became infected again. Thus began a series of operations and recurrent infections. Post-operation I was usually in absolute agony, and I recall much time spent in bed crying with pain.

During this time one person was a tremendous comfort to me – Jim Palmer, pastor of our local Assemblies of God church. He would come and visit regularly to pray for me. I remember how he ministered to me patiently and compassionately, praying for healing. He was very much like Jesus for me, a constant comfort.

After many more operations my wound eventually healed, but my problems were far from over. My leg became increasingly swollen and the doctors suspected this was probably lymphoedema – a serious swelling caused by occlusion of the lymphatic system. From my ongoing medical studies I knew that there was only really one surgeon in the UK who was an expert in lymphatics – Professor John B. Kinmonth, author of a then famous book, *Lymphatics: Diseases, Lymphography and Surgery*. My local library tracked down a copy for me and it became my new favourite book. At those times when my leg was worse, I would regularly be taken to see a local surgeon. It became apparent that he knew a great deal less about the condition than I did, because he hadn't read the book and I had!

On 5 September 1979 I was fifteen years old and in London for the day to watch the funeral procession of the assassinated Earl Mountbatten of Burma. I stood for hours in a prominent position by Westminster Abbey. By the time the ceremony had finished, my leg had swollen up so much that I was in agony and could hardly walk. Across the Thames I could see St Thomas' Hospital, and I decided I should take myself over to its A&E department to see what they could do for me.

I made it with some effort and, after looking at me, the doctors decided I ought to be admitted. I phoned home to tell my parents and a few hours later my mother arrived, bringing everything I would need. I was placed under the care of the orthopaedic department. I lay on my hospital bed thinking, "Why on earth am I in the orthopaedic department?" The next day the orthopaedic consultant came to see me. I remember him well: his name was Fred Heatley, and in just a few years I would be working alongside him. He looked at my leg and said, "You are in the right hospital but the wrong department." I knew that already! But then I was told I was being transferred to the care of Professor J. B. Kinmonth. My eyes lit up – the right man! I recall saying, "At last, the person I really need to see."

I wish I could say that this solved all my problems and that I was shortly made better, but things didn't turn out that way and there ensued a long, complex process. Prof. Kinmonth decided that there was a problem with the lymph nodes in my groin and that they should operate. To cut a long story short, it turned out that the groin had many infected nodes and, once again, post-operation the wound broke down. Multiple operations followed and at one point I was in hospital for fourteen consecutive weeks.

This scenario continued, not just for months but for years. In between operations I would go home, resume my schooling, and try to live life as normally as possible. On one occasion I became very ill and was losing consciousness. It was discovered that I had developed septicaemia. My situation was so grave that the hospital was unsure if I would survive. The consultant stood at the end of my bed telling my mother that my condition was so serious, he didn't know if I would pull through, but he would do everything possible to help me. I had my eyes closed as if I were asleep, but I could hear every word. I remember the occasion well, as it happened on 29 July 1981 and coincided with the marriage of Prince Charles to Lady Diana Spencer.

Eventually, I returned home and each day the district nurse came to dress my wounds before I left for school. Soon after this episode a surgeon decided to do a very radical procedure which involved removing a large section of the bottom of my abdomen and much of the top of my right leg. It was painful surgery, but it worked.

HOPE DASHED AND REBORN

Finally free of infection and back at school, I had to take my final exams. I was studying biology, chemistry, religious studies, and politics. A lot of the studying for these subjects I'd had to do on my own from my hospital bed. At this stage it was also time to apply to a university for further study.

There was no doubt about what I wanted to do – study anaesthetics and surgery. During my extensive reading I had obtained some valuable information. If one were to take the normal route for doing this, it would take years before one got to work in an operating theatre. But there was a way that would get you into the heart of the action very quickly, and that was training as an Operating Department Practitioner. Most of the teaching hospitals had training schools for this profession, so I applied to many prestigious establishments, but truly there was only one that I was really passionate about: St Thomas' Hospital, where I had spent a great deal of time as a patient. It was the oldest hospital in the country, with its roots dating back as far as 1106, and I loved its ethos. I prayed very hard that I might be able to train there.

I was eventually called for an interview at St Thomas'. When the day came I felt that the interview had gone wonderfully well and I loved my short time there. From then on, I monitored our letter box daily, waiting for a reply. Eventually a letter arrived, but to my utter dismay it said that unfortunately I had not been selected. Having prayed a great deal about it, I was certain that God had told me I would go there, so I couldn't understand why I'd been turned down. I was in despair and cried out to Him asking why.

At this time the head of sixth form at my school was a wonderful man called Michael Amos. I knew him fairly well, as I was the chair of the sixth-form committee. I had already told him of my desire to study at St Thomas' and so I shared with him my disappointment at being turned down. He was very encouraging and assured me that I would end up in the best place for me.

Just a few days later, as I was about to go out for the day, the postman arrived and handed me a letter. It was another piece of correspondence from St Thomas' Hospital, which was puzzling. I opened it and to my shock and delight it said that their previous letter had been an administrative error and I had in fact been selected for training, which would begin in September, subject to the successful completion of my exams. It was the happiest day of my life.

I showed the letter to Mr Amos the following Monday morning and he was thrilled. He hugged me and told me, "You are going to go very far and no one will be able to stop you."

Michael Amos was an inspirational man. I saw him again, just a few years ago, when I was awarded a major peace prize by the Wolf Institute at Cambridge University. The prize was presented to me by Baroness Valerie Amos, a senior member of the House of Lords and the current UN Under-Secretary-General for Humanitarian Affairs and Emergency Relief Coordinator. Baroness Amos is Michael's daughter and he was there to see me receive the prize. It gave me so much joy to see him, all these years later, and to be able to tell him what an inspiration he'd been to me.

Just a few weeks after the event, Baroness Amos contacted me to say her father was critically ill and dying. I returned from Iraq and was by his side in the UK until he died. Then I had the privilege of taking his funeral service. I can honestly say that, to me, it was one of the most important services I have ever taken.

Chapter 3

Just Like Heaven

I eventually took my exams and passed them well. September arrived with much anticipation and excitement on my part and I began my training at St Thomas' Hospital.

Being a student there was wonderful. My greatest dream had come true and there was no aspect of my study that I did not enjoy. During my early days at St Thomas' I lived at home and took an early train into London each morning.

To begin with, my time was spent only in the lecture theatre, but eventually the day came when we were allowed to pay a visit to the operating theatre and, for me at least, the really exciting part began. Special provision had to be made for my large size-sixteen feet. None of the available theatre boots would fit me and it took the hospital several months to track down a suitable pair for me. They had been specially made. I will never forget the first day I stepped into the theatre: the smell, the intense atmosphere... I always say it was like being in heaven, except that I'm sure heaven does not have all that blood.

Before I go further, I would point out that this chapter contains references to the medical procedures I was involved in performing – some of which are not for the squeamish. You have been warned!

* * *

My first six-week placement was working in anaesthesia, an area which continued to fascinate me, but my first proper theatre training was in urology and gynaecology – to my mind not the most interesting type of surgery. However, I loved being in the theatre. I was so enthusiastic to learn that in between cases I went off into the other theatres to observe the more dramatic procedures – orthopaedic, cardiac, or general surgery. Apparently this was not allowed, and it wasn't long until I was found out. I was severely reprimanded and told that students were not allowed to do this kind of thing!

So I spent a good deal of my time sitting in the dark, wet room that was the urology theatre. Most of the surgery was transurethral and was carried out with the surgeon sitting between the patient's legs with one eye glued to a uroscope. The person's bladder would be completely filled with water, then emptied again and again. The water came straight out onto the floor and was constantly mopped into the theatre's drains. Now you understand why it was both dark and wet. Eventually I would change to orthopaedic surgery, which was so much more enjoyable. Replacing a person's hip joint involved a lot of hammering and chiselling – much noisier than urology, but certainly a lot more fun (for me, not the patient). Meanwhile, I was learning much about the practical application of anaesthetics, though I already knew the theory inside out.

A regular visitor to the theatre was Suzy Lupton (now Knight), who was a student nurse on the men's urology ward and regularly brought down patients for their operations. Suzy was a Christian and we would also see each other at the hospital's Christian Union (CU) meetings. We became firm friends and over thirty years later our friendship remains as strong as it was then.

The CU was the major focal point for Christians studying at the hospital. It was almost, but not quite, entirely made up of students. They were a diverse bunch from across the hospital's many departments – medical students, student nurses at the Nightingale School of Nursing, students of pharmacy, radiology, physiotherapy, laboratory science, and phlebotomy, and Operating Department Practitioners like me.

The CU was very dynamic. We prayed, we sang, we had regular house parties and a whole series of excellent speakers. We were so much more than a group of Christians who met each week for a kind of service – deep friendships were forged and we continued to meet throughout the week in the library or staff restaurant. Many of us also attended the same churches.

It was in the CU that I met the closest male friend I have ever had, Malcolm Mathew. Malcolm was a medical student and we would see each other regularly at CU and around the hospital. Each Sunday Malcolm and I would go into the hospital again in order to take people in wheelchairs or beds to the chapel. It was a wonderful opportunity for us to have some meaningful contact with the patients and to take them to share in worship in the beautiful, traditional old Anglican chapel, which was the size of most decent parish churches.

The Chaplain, Michael Stevens, was a real friend to us and was widely loved and respected. Once a month he would invite the CU to take the chapel service and we students would lead the meeting. It was at one such service that I preached my first ever sermon. I confess it was a pretty awful sermon, but it was the beginning of what would turn into a lifetime of preaching. I immediately realized I needed much more public-speaking experience, so after chapel and lunch Malcolm and I would often go to Speakers' Corner in Hyde Park and I would speak on a mixture of faith and politics.

Most Sundays, a stint at Speakers' Corner was followed by a Tube ride to the church that many of our fellow CU members attended, St Mark's, Kennington. St Mark's was a powerhouse of a church, where the Charismatic community met the established church, resulting in a vibrant atmosphere. The vicar was Nicholas Rivett-Carnac, a man full to overflowing with the Holy Spirit and the love of God, as was his lovely wife, Marigold. They were both adored by the congregation.

An experience of God's Spirit

Attending St Mark's was a great experience for all of us students. It was like a machine that recharged our batteries at the end of each week. Though I had grown up with some experience of the Pentecostal Church, I had never before spent a long time in a dynamic, Spirit-filled environment. I was aware of the experience of the "infilling of the Holy Spirit" that is at the heart of Pentecostal Christian teaching, but I had not experienced this myself.

In our old Assemblies of God church we would regularly have "waiting meetings" in which we would sit, pray, and wait to be filled with the Holy Spirit – the evidence of which would be the gift of speaking in tongues. I confess that these were among the most boring meetings I have ever attended. They were certainly about waiting – we waited and waited and did little else. I do not want to generalize, of course, but the small part of the Pentecostal Church that I knew personally had changed much since the days of Smith Wigglesworth and become set in its ways. At St Mark's, however, I experienced a taste of the glory and power of God as never before.

The day came when I realized that I needed someone to pray for me, in order for me to experience the Holy Spirit in this new way. At one particular meeting I went and knelt at the altar, and a dear lady called Anthea Demitri prayed for me. That day my life was changed for ever. The presence of the Holy Spirit hit me like a thunderbolt. Although I wasn't expecting it, I received the gift of speaking in tongues, and from that moment on I was a new man. That night I went home singing and glorifying God loudly in tongues.

I noticed the difference the next day when I went into St Thomas'. It was a theatre training day, rather than lectures, and as I entered the theatre I was aware, as never before, of the glory and presence of God. It was quite amazing.

My physiology lecturer was the very interesting and totally eccentric Louis Cronje. If a student answered a question correctly during his lecture he would give them a Jelly Baby™. This day he came right up to me during class, planted his hands on my desk, looked me in the eyes, and said, "Andrew, you are going to do very well here, but this is not where you are meant to be. You are going to change the world." This was remarkable in itself, but he went on to repeat this mantra to me week in and week out for months to come. I didn't want to change the world. I just wanted to become a good "gas man", as anaesthetists are known.

One of the surgeons I had the privilege of assisting was Ian Fergusson. I helped him with a number of caesarean section births and he told me that I was his favourite student for such tasks, since I had such large hands and was best at helping the baby out. Until he'd said that, I hadn't realized I had such big hands; I just knew I had big feet!

It was a huge responsibility to help bring a new life into the world, but I now knew the constant reassuring presence of the Holy Spirit and this helped me to cope with potentially difficult or stressful situations. On another occasion, I was assigned to help a visiting surgeon from India in the cardiac theatre. The patient was having a new aortic valve fitted, but the surgeon put it in the wrong way. As a result I spent the next four hours holding a retractor in the heart while the mistake was corrected, and it meant I had to keep as steady as a rock. Before long I was in agony, but I just could not move and jeopardize the procedure. I silently praised and worshipped God and, somehow, He sustained me and got me through it.

It was a wonder to me how intertwined my spiritual life was with my medical life and I had many wonderful times of praise and worship on my own in operating theatres while I was doing the set-up and preparation. Anyone looking in on me may well have thought I was mad!

A BUMP IN THE ROAD

I was well into my training when suddenly I developed some pain and swelling in my right groin. Within a day my old wound had totally broken down and I was in a bad way. I was admitted to St Thomas' as a patient and placed on a staff ward. This was very different from being a "normal" patient, since I knew all the staff and had worked with many of them.

By this time I had a great deal more knowledge and knew enough to understand how complex and dangerous my situation was. A date was set for surgery, this time carried out by friends/colleagues. I had the surgery and we waited to see the outcome, but it was only a matter of days before the wound broke down and became infected again. Several more operations followed and I began to worry about all the study time I was missing. Eventually I was sent home to my parents and told to allow enough time to recuperate properly.

By now I had moved out of the family home and a couple of fellow students and I were living in rented accommodation. Returning home was not easy. My sister, Joanna, though now engaged, was still suffering very much and was extremely hard to be around. My brother, Mark, who was by far the most intelligent of all of us, had finished school but opted out of going to university. Instead, his only interests seemed to be football and hanging out with a crowd of very unsavoury characters. His behaviour was erratic and I became convinced that he was taking drugs. Increasingly, he was getting into trouble with the police.

After a period of rest I was well enough to return to St Thomas' and found it difficult to leave such a complex family situation behind. Given my brother's and sister's situations, I was profoundly conscious, despite my health problems, of how blessed I was to be thriving in an environment I loved, and keenly aware of God's presence with me. I did not take it for granted. But I also wondered why it was that both my brother and my sister were suffering with their mental well-being and I was not. It's something that I still do not understand.

On my return to St Thomas' I decided to become as fit as I could and so became a vegetarian and began running several miles every day. Within a short while I felt the healthiest I had ever been and, of course, loved being back at the hospital. My academic work was going well, but the teaching staff came to the conclusion that, because of all the time I'd lost while I'd been hospitalized and then recuperating, my training would have to be extended, and my finals were put back three months. But, once again, I knew God's help. I completed my thesis in obstetric problems and, when I eventually took my exams, I got excellent results.

To the north and back

After qualifying I was appointed to my first proper role in obstetric anaesthetics at Derby City Hospital, and headed north into a very different world from that which I'd known in London.

Here my work spanned both the operating theatre and the labour ward, and so involved epidurals as much as caesarean sections. The hospital was radically different from St Thomas' and I longed to be back in London. At the earliest opportunity I applied for a new job there and to my delight I was accepted. After my brief foray to the north I was soon back in my beloved St Thomas' and working in my favourite theatres again.

I was tasked with dealing with three main areas. The first was any emergency surgery that needed doing. Emergencies occurred daily, but we dealt with the issues that were too complex to be handled by other hospitals. Second was vascular surgery – venous, arterial, and lymphatic – dealing with radical problems such as aortic aneurisms. Third, there was ear, nose, and throat surgery (ENT). ENT probably doesn't sound very challenging to most people, but from an anaesthetic and surgical point of view it can be very demanding indeed, including as it does such procedures as laryngectomy (removing the voice box in cancer patients). There were also many paediatric cases, and anaesthetizing children is always very difficult.

These were the delights I faced on a daily basis, but increasingly I was asked to become involved in the hospital's "crash team" as well. This is essentially the cardiac arrest team, but they are usually called on to assist with other major crises in the A&E department. The crash team were a full-time unit, but I was seconded to the team whenever they needed extra capacity. I soon found myself volunteering for them, even when I was not on duty, and would come in to support them at weekends. It meant carrying around a crash bleeper and, when an emergency occurred, the miniature screen flashed up "Crash call" with the location of the event. One would then run there as fast as possible and try to resuscitate the patient. When I tell people about these events today I like to say that I didn't just put people to sleep, I also raised the dead!

During my training one lecturer uttered a phrase that has always stayed with me: "Medicine," he said, "must never become torture." There were times when I wondered whether our treatment of patients was indeed treatment or torture. Sometimes the "treatment" could be radical and painful. If the damage didn't cause long-term problems, then this was acceptable. But, at times, saving a person's life meant leaving them in a terrible state for the rest of that life.

Don't read on unless you can cope with something seriously gruesome, but the worst case I ever dealt with was when we were called to assist a man who had been crushed under a stage lift at the National Theatre in London. After he was extracted, his treatment meant almost daily surgery, which included amputating both his legs. Then, one day, it was decided that he needed a hemicorporectomy – the complete amputation of the lower half of the body from above the pelvis. It was the most horrendous operation I have ever seen and I admit to praying that he would not survive. Towards the end of his surgery he went into cardiac arrest and my colleagues and I agreed that we could not resuscitate him. Medicine had become torture, rather than the healing and restoring process it was meant to be. The Lord gives and the Lord takes away, but sometimes we try to stop Him. Medical ethics, I believe, are as much about not going too far as about not going far enough.

So life at St Thomas' was busy and demanding, but I thrived in that environment. "This is it," I thought. "I'll probably spend the rest of my career right here." But I was wrong.

CHAPTER 4

Called by God

One day, between crash calls, I was standing in the hospital gardens opposite Big Ben and praying. I began to thank God for everything He had done for me. He had enabled me to both train and now work at St Thomas'. He had built a wonderful spiritual foundation in my life and filled me with His presence. Then I said to Him, "What next, Lord?" and presumed He would say I should stay right where I was and that one day I would become the crash team director. But He did not. Instead, He said very clearly, "I want you to go into the Church of England."

Immediately I protested: "But I love it here. You sent me here and I'm good at what I do. Besides, they are not even all saved in the Church of England!"

But when God calls you to do something, you cannot fight it for long. He always gets His own way and He spent the following day changing my mind.

The next morning I was preparing for that day's cases in theatre and entered into what was now my regular time of praise and worship. As I did so, I became increasingly aware of the fact that all I actually wanted to do with my life was to serve God. I wanted to do what He wanted me to do – even if it meant training for ministry in the Church of England. As the day wore on, I felt more and more that, in fact, I did want to go into the church.

Near the end of the day we performed a procedure on a patient to bypass a blocked artery in their leg and, by the end of it, I wanted nothing more than to serve God through His church. Then the Lord brought to my mind the question I'd been asked as a ten-year-old boy: "What do you want to do when you grow up?", to which I had responded, "Work in anaesthetics and be a priest." I had done the first; maybe now I was going to do the second.

It was clear that all this was from God. He had given me the desires of my heart in the first place. I needed to talk to someone about all this and so went to my vicar at St Mark's, Nicholas, and earnestly told him what I felt God was saying. I didn't realize at the time that vicars are regularly accosted by people telling them they think they are being called to ministry, so I didn't quite get the reaction I was hoping for. Instead, he graciously passed me over to Mike Marshall, his new curate, to talk me through the process.

I met with Mike to discuss things. He began by asking if I was really qualified enough to cope with training for ministry. Had I been to university? Did I have a degree in anything? I assured him that I had a degree in surgery and anaesthetics from St Thomas' Hospital. He told me that selection for ministry was a long process that began with a meeting with the Director of Ordinands and could last for up to two years. In due course this would culminate in a three-day residential selection conference, from which recommendations would be given to the diocesan bishop regarding who should train for ordination.

Undeterred by the length of the process or the fact that I might be turned down at the end, I pressed ahead and had a series of meetings with Canon John Cox. He could see how much I loved my present job, but that I was also very committed to wanting to serve God and His people. I was rightly pushed hard to consider the tension between my intense love for the medical world and the major sacrifice it would be to leave that way of life. But things progressed well and it was not long before I was told I needed to begin thinking about where I would study theology. I was informed that I should consider Oxford or Cambridge. I was excited by this. In my heart I would always have loved to be an Oxbridge scholar, and here was my chance.

I thought that Oxford was perhaps the better place and began to investigate some of the Oxford colleges. But another of my close friends at St Thomas' was a student nurse called Maria and she was from Cambridge – her father was a Methodist minister who had trained there. Maria decided she was taking me to Cambridge and I immediately fell in love with both the city and its university.

While there, I recalled a school trip to Cambridge years before, when I was a small boy. I'd walked down King's Parade and said to myself, "Oh, I wish I could come and study here one day." It seemed destined that God would bring me here.

I was very blessed whilst at St Mark's, Kennington to be in a wonderful home group led by Ray and Carol Austin. I had first met Ray on the cardiothoracic operating table. He had an inoperable bronchial tumour. He was a young man and it was an issue of major concern to the thoracic team. To cut a very long story short, his wife got him back home from hospital and Nicholas, the vicar of St Mark's, came round to pray for him. Ray returned to hospital for checks a completely healed man. Ray and Carol were a massive encouragement and support to me as I toiled through the laborious selection process.

Finally, I was put forward for the selection conference known as ACCM (the Advisory Council for the Church's Ministry). As I began to prepare for the conference, I had a sudden revelation: I was not actually an Anglican! I had never been confirmed as a member of the Church of England. So it was swiftly arranged for me to have an emergency confirmation at a church in Croydon. I became an Anglican just four days before I went to the selection conference!

Once I had got to this stage I had to be honest with the hospital about the possibility of my moving to Cambridge to study theology in preparation for going into the Church of England. All my colleagues were shocked by this news, but every one of them was very supportive. It was interesting to see that the response from my family was quite different. They could not understand how I could turn my back on my wonderful training and the place where I had always wanted to work, especially to go into the Church of England. They were ardent Nonconformists; was their son joining the opposition?

The day came for the final selection conference. It was at Bishop Woodford House in Ely – a wonderful setting for probably the most important interview of my life. There were sixteen people being interviewed from all over the UK. None of us knew each other. Then there was a considerable interviewing panel with each person looking at a different aspect of ministry. The chair was an archdeacon from Leicestershire and, to my surprise, I discovered that he had also been a Strict Baptist, like me. I remember one question he asked: "What is the most inspirational book you have read recently?" I had just read William Temple's *Philosophy of Religion,* which was excellent, but was not the book that had really inspired me. The book that had challenged and motivated me most was a little book by Colin Urquhart, who regularly preached at St Mark's, called *Anything You Ask.* It was simply about putting faith into action. I mentioned this and we had a brief discussion about living in the dimension of God's miraculous power. It was an unusual line to take for one wanting to be a part of the state church.

I returned to London full of expectation and waited impatiently for a response. My operating theatre colleagues seemed as keen to hear the answer as I was. Eventually the letter arrived at my flat in Kennington and it said that the bishop was recommending me for training for ordination. I looked at my diary and planned to use some of my holiday leave for spiritual preparation for my training. I was scheduled to spend a week at Colin Urquhart's Kingdom Faith Conference, where I had pledged my services to look after the on-site medical centre. After that I thought I would go and spend some time in a monastery. The Kingdom Faith week was outstanding and in both the ministry times and the medical clinic we saw lots of miracles. It was a wonderful time – apart from the camping. I have never had the calling to be a camper!

Afterwards I went home to visit my parents before returning to work, and found them in a frenzy. They had been trying to contact me for three days (this was long before the ubiquity of mobile phones). The hospital wanted me urgently. They had major problems with their crash team: a member of staff had been suspended, and I was to be appointed temporary director.

I returned to St Thomas' and threw myself into this task. I loved every minute of it. I had wanted to be director of the crash team one day and here I was, being given a taste of what it was like. I was given accommodation in the hospital itself because of the importance of the role. Here I was experiencing another taste of heaven, but, of course, it could not continue. In due course I would leave and train to be a priest. Through this, however, God helped me to realize something very important. What was it that I loved most about the crash team? It was rising to the occasion of dealing with a crisis. One day, all this training in dealing with crises under pressure would be immensely valuable to me – as valuable as my spiritual training.

I had thought I might take a few days' break between finishing at St Thomas' and going to Cambridge, but this was not to be. Until the very day before I left for Cambridge I was working – and that day was as busy as ever. My bleeper went off and I was called to a cardiac arrest in the psychiatric outpatients department.

It was not an area of the hospital the crash team expected to visit frequently and I knew that the resuscitation equipment there would be very limited, so I grabbed the nearest anaesthetic machine and ran with it down the corridor to the psychiatric unit. Just then, one of the senior nursing officers got in my way and I swerved to avoid knocking her flying. As I did so, the anaesthetic machine hit me in the face, chipping my teeth, and blood began pouring down my chin. Fortunately, we managed to resuscitate the patient and all was well – apart from my smashed-up face. The next day I took the train to Cambridge and began my training for ordination looking as if I had just lost a fist fight. Whoever would believe what had happened to me?

CHAPTER 5

The Academic Hothouse

I arrived in Cambridge with my battered face (to more than a few bemused stares) and found my accommodation. I liked my room off H staircase at Ridley Hall. I was shocked when I opened the wardrobe in the study and discovered a list, to which each of the room's former occupants had added their name. It included many of the great leaders of our faith tradition, such as John Stott and David Watson, and now here I was too.

I joined the other new students to attend an induction talk and was pleased to hear that I would be learning not just theology, but also philosophy, church history, Greek, liturgy, and much more. Then we had our pre-term lecture. This was a special event at which a significant visiting speaker would address all the new students. We had the privilege of listening to Bishop Lesslie Newbigin, who had spent much of his ministry serving as a missionary in India. I remember thinking what a tremendous sacrifice he had made to do this.

Soon the term proper began and I was surprised to find that the academic discipline required was much more demanding than I'd expected. I found the study very difficult, but nonetheless pursued it with joy. I suppose I was experiencing the phenomenon common to postgraduates: the discomfort of being "deskilled". Most of the students had come from places where they had been pretty good at something – perhaps even expert at it. My discipline had been medicine and surgery. But, now, whatever we'd previously been very good at didn't matter. We were nobodies! I guess the undergraduates experienced this too, but in a different way. Most of them would have been the outstanding students in their former institutions, and suddenly they were among hundreds of other students who were just as brilliant. Such paradoxes exist at places like Oxford and Cambridge, where everybody is very gifted.

In parallel with our academic work, we learned about the pastoral side of ministry. Each of us was assigned to a parish. I was blessed to be attached to one of the most significant, historic churches in Cambridge, Holy Trinity. It was the church where the famous English evangelical Charles Simeon had been vicar. Simeon had also been the Dean of King's College and was hailed as one of the great early evangelical preachers. For me, being a part of Simeon's church was one of the best things about being in Cambridge.

There have been many books written about Simeon, but one of his recorded discussions with John Wesley best sums up the man and his beliefs:

> *[Speaking to an elderly John Wesley] Sir, I understand that you are called an Arminian; and I have been sometimes called a Calvinist; and therefore I suppose we are to draw daggers. But before I consent to begin the combat, with your permission I will ask you a few questions. Pray, Sir, do you feel yourself a depraved*

creature, so depraved that you would never have thought of turning to God, if God had not first put it into your heart?

Yes, I do indeed.

And do you utterly despair of recommending yourself to God by anything you can do; and look for salvation solely through the blood and righteousness of Christ?

Yes, solely through Christ.

But, Sir, supposing you were at first saved by Christ, are you not somehow or other to save yourself afterwards by your own works?

No, I must be saved by Christ from first to last.

Allowing, then, that you were first turned by the grace of God, are you not in some way or other to keep yourself by your own power?

No.

What then, are you to be upheld every hour and every moment by God, as much as an infant in its mother's arms?

Yes, altogether.

And is all your hope in the grace and mercy of God to preserve you unto His heavenly kingdom?

53

Yes, I have no hope but in Him.

*Then, Sir, with your leave I will put up my dagger
again; for this is all my Calvinism; this is my election,
my justification by faith, my final perseverance: it is in
substance all that I hold, and as I hold it; and therefore,
if you please, instead of searching out terms and phrases
to be a ground of contention between us, we will
cordially unite in those things where in we agree.[3]*

As one formed very much within the Calvinist tradition, I
have a great affinity with all that Simeon stood for. I was
simply awed to be able to serve in the same parish in which
he served.

THE DAWNING OF MY RECONCILIATION WORK

Along with the inspiration I drew from Simeon, and the
history of his former church, I was also impressed and
inspired by its new curate. David Armstrong from Northern
Ireland had just been installed after being a Presbyterian
minister for many years. During his time in Northern Ireland
he had steadfastly refused to be drawn into the sectarian
divide between Catholics and Protestants.

In his book, *Road Too Wide*,[4] he tells the story of how, one
Christmas, he walked across a road that marked the religious
territorial divide, just to say happy Christmas to some
Catholics. The resulting fallout was unbelievably horrendous.
David's example was my first introduction to the concept of

---

3   Moule, Handley, *Charles Simeon – Pastor of a Generation*, Christian Focus
Publications, 2005, page 79 ff.
4   Armstrong, David, *Road Too Wide*, Marshall Pickering, 1985.

the ministry of reconciliation. I learned so much from him about the value of taking risks and showing love to others for the sake of peace. Little did I know that one day this would be the all-consuming focus of my work and life.

After three years David moved to be vicar of another church in the poorer end of Cambridge, and I decided to go with him. I was with him throughout my four years in Cambridge and he imparted much wisdom to me. One extremely useful piece of advice he gave me was this: "Don't ever read your sermons or use notes; look at the people." To this day I have always observed this practice. During my time at college and also through my curacy I was forced to use notes, mainly because they were checked by our superiors, but once I was a free man I never used them again. It is so important to look into people's eyes, engage with them, read their reactions, and respond accordingly.

A GROWING INTEREST IN JUDAISM

My studies continued to challenge me so much more than my medical studies had, but two subjects that I found thoroughly enjoyable were Judaism and the Philosophy of Religion. In addition to my compulsory lectures I would often go and listen to one of the most inspiring lecturers at Cambridge at that time, Rabbi Professor Nicholas de Lange. I learned a great deal from him. I admired the fact that he didn't just "lecture", but taught like a real rabbi.

My interest in Judaism continued to grow such that in due course I became a member of Cambridge's Jewish Society. I wanted to deepen my understanding of how the Jewish faith supplied the foundation of our Christian faith. I even began attending the weekly Friday evening service at the local Orthodox Synagogue and stayed on for the meal after the service. The Jewish community became as much "my community" as the Christian church.

I continued to feel somewhat deskilled and missed my medical career. Once I could do practical things that had an immediate, positive effect on people and often radically changed their life. Now I would study, attend lectures, and write, write, write! It was a challenge, but I told myself I was working towards something bigger.

Then life changed drastically for me again when I started to become quite ill. Gradually at first, then increasingly, I noticed that I had multiple troubling symptoms of some form of illness, including a number of quite serious neurological symptoms. These began to worsen and I was eventually admitted to Addenbrooke's Hospital. I stayed there for two weeks, feeling very ill, before I was moved into the Principal's Lodge for a short time until it could be arranged to send me home to my parents. I can't describe how awful I felt. A number of consultations ensued and it was thought that I had myalgic encephalomyelitis, commonly known simply as ME.

At my parents', I lay in bed for the next two weeks, feeling so ill that I could hardly get up to go to the bathroom. Long before I was really ready, I returned to Cambridge, determined to get on with my studies. Back at Cambridge I was not well enough to sit through an entire lecture, so my lecturers would come to me each day, courtesy of the Cambridge system in which much of the important work is carried out by means of one-to-one supervisions.

At the time, if someone had told me that these symptoms would remain with me for the majority of my foreseeable life and ministry, I would not have believed them – but that was to be the case. And yet, through God's grace and

His strength, I have never been unable to do anything I have needed to do. There were certainly those around me who wondered if I would ever be well enough to fulfil the duties of a curate, but I remain grateful to the then Bishop of Kingston, Peter Selby, who insisted I could do all I would ever need to do.

Meanwhile, the single most significant event of my time in Cambridge was about to happen.

PEACEMAKER

The Christian presence in Cambridge has always been very strong, and was led by the Cambridge Inter-Collegiate Christian Union (CICCU). Every three years CICCU had a big mission. In 1988 the mission was chaired by a good friend of mine, Richard Coombs. Richard lived in the room next to mine and, in years to come, would be best man at my wedding. This year, the mission committee decided to invite Jews for Jesus to participate in order to "target" as many Jewish students as possible. At this point the whole venture began to go horribly wrong, as the Jewish community learned about the plans and was up in arms about it.

As the only Christian who was also a member of a synagogue, I was asked if I would intervene in this crisis. As a measure of just how serious the matter was, the headline of the *Jewish Chronicle* read, "Holy War in Cambridge". How was the situation going to be resolved? What was clear was that we had to get the Jews and Christians talking to one another. This was a lot more complex than it sounds. I took on responsibility for dealing with the issue.

I spent a long time talking to the CICCU leadership about the fears of the Jewish community. They didn't really understand. In their eyes, their priority was simply to get people saved and keep them out of hell. They could not grapple with the many theological questions about the role of the Jews in soteriology.

When I sat down with the Jews, their attitude was very different. They expressed their awareness of the history of their people, not least of how, in the past, they had suffered forced conversion at the hands of "militant Christians". They were particularly anxious about this group, Jews for Jesus – who came from the Christian understanding of Messianic Judaism. Classical Judaism is Messianic at its heart, but always rooted in the future.

What was clear from my meetings with both parties was the possibility of a complete breakdown of relationship between the two. What needed to happen was a meeting of representatives from the two communities who were willing to engage with one another. I managed to call together a meeting of those Jews and Christians who were willing to start a dialogue.

I found that whereas many Orthodox Jewish students were willing to participate, far fewer evangelical Christians were keen to engage, so I reached out to students from a more liberal theological college, Westcott House, and some students from there became involved. In due course, it seemed appropriate to strengthen the foundations of this initial gathering and formalize it by starting a new society in the university. So began a group called Cambridge University Jews and Christians (CUJAC). The founding meeting was held at King's College, Cambridge and the speaker was Rabbi Jeremy Rosen, who was Chief Rabbi Jakobovits's cabinet member for interfaith affairs. It was a great meeting attended by over 100 people – Jews and Christians drawn from undergraduates and postgraduates as well as college fellows.

What we had begun was a unique process of reconciliation. Here was something that had no official place in my study programme at Cambridge, yet it was foundational in preparing me for the bulk of my work in years to come – where I would spend the majority of my time seeking reconciliation between opposing groups. CUJAC went from strength to strength, meeting not just occasionally but up to three times each week during term time. Lectures, text studies, visits to different places of worship, and visiting speakers were all part of our regular routine.

It was only a matter of weeks before CUJAC was asked to become involved with the Council of Christians and Jews (CCJ). The oldest interfaith organization in the UK, it was established during World War II by the then Archbishop of Canterbury, William Temple, and Chief Rabbi, Joseph H. Hertz. I decided I should get involved with them and a short while later was offered an honorary role on their executive. That summer the international branch of the CCJ, based in Heppenheim, Germany, was to hold its annual meeting in England. This included a meeting of its young leadership section. Each year, young people from around the world who were committed to Jewish–Christian relations would come together to discuss the issue. Somehow I found myself dragged into organizing a somewhat badly planned meeting at the last minute. I rather enjoyed this, bringing order out of chaos at the drop of a hat.

The ICCJ's young leadership section had an international committee and, towards the end of the conference, they elected people to be committee members for the next two years. To my utter surprise, since I was very new to the movement, I was elected. To my even greater surprise, I was then unanimously voted in as chairman. It was an important step that would set me on the road to my ultimate destiny.

CHAPTER 6

A Prophetic Word

FORMER ARCHBISHOP'S INFLUENCE

My new role as Chairman of the ICCJ was very high-profile. It carried with it a seat on the board of the organization's international council. By virtue of becoming chairman I also got to know one of the most inspirational people I've ever known: Donald, Lord Coggan, former Archbishop of Canterbury and the Honorary President of the movement. He quickly became my teacher and mentor.

I would see Lord Coggan at ICCJ meetings around the world and also visit him regularly in the UK, in Cambridge or London or at his home in Winchester, where he lived with his dear wife, Jean. When in London, we would often meet at the home of two other great friends, Sidney and Elizabeth Corob. Sidney was a statesman of the Jewish community and a great businessman and philanthropist. Lord Coggan and I would often sit talking with Sidney and Elizabeth in their Mayfair home. I frequently wondered why on earth these two men should invest so much of their valuable time in a young man like me, who hadn't really achieved anything.

Thankfully, they saw something bigger – they were investing in a future generation.

As I left the house in Hill Street, Mayfair, Lord Coggan would always take my hand and hold it tight in order to get my full attention. He would tell me how radical leaders of the church needed to be and how I must never compromise in my leadership of our Lord's church. I pray that I have never compromised and I have always tried to keep my promise to Lord Coggan – and, more importantly, to the Lord Himself.

Visits to St Thomas'

When I was not attending ICCJ events, and despite having continuing health problems, I would return to help at St Thomas's Hospital. I was not well enough to cope with the rigours of the crash team, running around the hospital resuscitating the dead, but I could work in anaesthetics in the operating theatre. Acting as a medical locum meant that I managed to earn quite a lot of money during my Cambridge days and thus didn't have to be a poor student.

During the summer I worked through a well-respected agency. I knew little about the company other than that the CEO was someone called Dr Baker. Many years later, this "Dr Baker" would become one of my closest colleagues in the war zone of Baghdad. It turned out he was none other than Dr Mowaffak Baqer al-Rubaie, who lived and worked in the UK until 2003, when he was appointed to the Iraqi Governing Council, and later to the role of National Security Advisor. In 2003 he contacted me to discuss his return to Iraq, knowing that I was involved there, but with no idea of our past link. I would eventually move into his house in

Baghdad and over a decade later we are still close colleagues and see each other at least once each week.

After the summer break I would return to Cambridge, inspired to face the challenges of the coming year. Each new academic year began with a Freshers' Fair. It was here that the many university societies would do their best to recruit new members. In 1989, the beginning of my final year, I was promoting CUJAC and had a great conversation with a young law student, Melanie Wright. She clearly had a huge interest in Jewish–Christian relations and ended up getting involved with us. In a matter of weeks she switched course from law to theology and in time she would become the president of CUJAC.

By now I was involved in some serious research and my subject was "The Role of Israel in Christian Theology". It was an area that brought together all of my major interests: Christianity, Judaism, and Israel. My three years of study at Cambridge had been extended, so I had the opportunity to go to spend some time in Israel, where I studied at the Hebrew University in Jerusalem. At the same time I was interviewing large numbers of Christians about their theological approach to Israel. It was a non-stop learning experience.

Apart from my general interest in Judaism, I had a specific interest in Hasidism, or "ultra-Orthodoxy". The followers of Hasidism are the most recognizable Jews – the men with the big fur hats and ringlets of hair hanging from their heads. Hasidic Jews, however, form a very closed community. Outsiders cannot easily engage with them in order to find out about their ideology. Hasidism was founded in eighteenth-century Eastern Europe by Rabbi Israel Baal Shem Tov in response to the *Haskalah* (the Jewish Enlightenment), when many Jews moved away from their traditional way of life, based on the traditional study of the Torah (Scripture), Talmud, and Mishnah (traditional Jewish writings).

I became friends with an ultra-Orthodox rabbi who expressed his concern about my studying Hasidism at the Hebrew University, which he viewed as being very liberal. He recognized my love of Judaism and wanted me to understand it really thoroughly. To my surprise, he offered to let me join his ultra-Orthodox yeshiva (seminary) in Mea Shearim, the Hasidic part of Jerusalem. I often say that going to yeshiva and marrying Caroline were the two most important things in my life. That is not to say that Cambridge was not influential – it was – but it was at Mea Shearim that I developed my immense love for Hasidism.

During my studies I lived with the Hasidic community and realized how diverse they are. Though the people look similar in appearance, each community grouping has its own name, usually linked to where it originated in Eastern Europe. There are at least fifty different groups, but among the ultra-Orthodox there is a major division between the Hasidim and the Misnagdim, which literally means "the opponents" of the Hasidim. The Misnagdim are also known as the Litvaks because they originate from Lithuania.

While the practice of Hasidism tends to look very serious and formal to outsiders, on Friday night after Shabbat the chief rabbis of each group host a celebration called the Tish (which literally means "table"). The men who attend these events sing and dance like most people could not comprehend! These events are never filmed because they happen on Shabbat, when it is forbidden to use cameras.

So, in this enclosed environment I literally lived Judaism. We could not speak Hebrew because it was seen as too holy to use as an everyday language for communication, so the old Jewish language of Eastern Europe was used, combining German, Russian, and some Hebrew, but the latter only in written form. This was not seen as a kosher community, but as a *glatt kosher* one. In other words, "extra-special kosher". When I finally got back to Cambridge I was appointed as the *kashrut* (kosher) officer to the Cambridge University Jewish Society. It was unheard of to have a *goy* (a non-Jew) overseeing *kashrut*. But then the Jewish students complained that I was too strict with them. Glatt kosher I was!

I remember the college principal approaching me one day and telling me not to be too Jewish and to remember that I was a Christian. I hadn't forgotten that I was, first and foremost, a Christian, but I was also very aware that my Master and Messiah, Jesus, was not a Christian but a Jew.

As I entered my final year at Cambridge plans had to be made for where I would serve my title. There seemed to be only one serious option: St Mark's Church in Battersea Rise. This was a church plant from Holy Trinity Church, Brompton, just over the river in central London, by far one of the most dynamic churches in the country. I very much wanted to go to St Mark's, but there were questions over whether I would be fit enough, on account of my health. Bishop Peter Selby intervened and said he felt I was the right person for the post, and so I was assigned there.

By God's grace I passed all my exams and I was scheduled for ordination. I was sad to be leaving Cambridge, but at the same time excited, because I planned to spend my summer back in Israel.

Two people wanted to accompany me that summer. The first was Melanie Wright, the former law student from the Freshers' Fair. The other was a friend from St Thomas'

Christian Union, Alison Boyle. We went to Israel together and had a wonderful time. It was so different from what my days in Israel would be like in just a few years' time. We stayed in the Maronite Hostel and lived on fruit and vegetables, travelled around Israel by bus, and spent a bit of time lying on the beach in Galilee.

We visited Jerusalem, where we met my ultra-Orthodox rabbi friend. As we stood chatting in the cobbled streets I was very surprised when he told me that he wanted me to meet someone very important, someone who, as he put it, was full of the glory of Adonai (the Lord).

"This person can speak the words of God to you," he told me. I could see that the rabbi was totally inspired by this person and I listened intently, expecting to hear the name of another prominent rabbi. Instead, he told me of a Christian who, like me, had a love and reverence for Judaism. More of a shock than that, this person was a woman, not a man. So this ultra-Orthodox rabbi sent me to meet a Christian lady called Ruth Heflin.

I didn't know who Ruth was, so I tried to find out. My circles in Jerusalem tended to be very Jewish, but I made contact with Christ Church, Jaffa Gate, an evangelical Anglican church. The people there gave me a very different impression. Ruth Heflin was described to me as "powerful and scary"! It turned out that she led a ministry called the Mount Zion Fellowship. They were based on the east side of Jerusalem, the predominantly Arab side, and every Saturday evening they held a meeting. That Saturday night my friends and I decided to go and visit this house in Nashashibi Street in East Jerusalem.

Having attended many Charismatic services, I had seen a few things that more-conservative believers might consider "wacky", but this meeting was in a completely different league. The service was powerful, however, and there was a tangible sense of God's presence there. The "powerful and scary" lady was certainly present in force. She led with power. She sang her own songs, prophesied, and preached on the glory of God. Many of those present had flown in from all over the world to attend and many had come simply to receive prayer for healing.

Suddenly, in the midst of all the action, Ruth stopped what she was doing and approached me and my friends. She pointed at me and actually shouted, "The Lord has called and chosen you to spend your life working for peace in the Middle East. Through you the Lord will do great things in this region."

That was it. I can remember thinking, "That's a nice prophetic word for a Saturday evening." Ruth then approached Melanie, who by nature was quite reserved, pointed at her, and said, "The Lord has chosen you to be a great academic leader in Jewish–Christian relations."

It was a remarkable evening and I thought much about what had happened. An ultra-Orthodox rabbi introducing me to a scary prophetic lady who had a razor-sharp word from the Lord could only have been orchestrated by the Lord Himself.

You may have noticed that I have not mentioned my rabbi friend's name. It is because our close friendship would not be understood by the Hasidic community and if this became public it could be very unhelpful for him. Before leaving Israel we visited him again and I told him what Ruth had said to me. I was really intrigued to know how he himself had come to know her. He told me that the reason for their friendship was simple: at heart, Ruth held to many of the Hasidic virtues of dynamism and mysticism. Suddenly I began to see the connection.

As I think about that meeting now, many years later, I am humbled by how Ruth's words have come to pass, for me and for my friend. Melanie did become a great academic on the subject of Jewish–Christian relations. She studied for her DPhil at Oxford, wrote a number of books, and returned to Cambridge to teach. I always maintained contact with her. Latterly, she became ill and was diagnosed with cancer. When she was terminally ill we kept in contact daily between Iraq and Cambridge via email. In the days before she died we suddenly started communicating about that crazy day in Jerusalem. She had never forgotten it either. Melanie reminded me that Ruth did not say I was to spend my life working for peace in "Israel" but "the Middle East". Today I am still involved in Israel but based in Arab Iraq. God knows what He is doing even if we do not! My dear Melanie passed to glory while still very young, but I will never forget her.

CHAPTER 7

Life-defining Events

My years of learning in the ivory tower of Cambridge were over and I entered the real world and began serving my title at St Mark's, Battersea Rise, sponsored by the Diocese of Southwark. Back in familiar territory, I took up this role with a great sense of joy and anticipation. I had roots in this area of south London, having worshipped at St Mark's, Kennington during my student days at St Thomas' Hospital.

St Mark's, Battersea Rise, was one of three church plants out of Holy Trinity, Brompton, the others being St Paul's, Onslow Square and St Barnabas, Kensington. Our vicar at St Mark's was Paul Perkin, a highly respected man who had been sent out to pioneer the church plant. Church planting in the Anglican Church tends to be different from other church streams. Whereas many churches aim to plant in areas where there is no church, and will meet in school halls and the like, C of E "plants" were all existing Anglican churches with significant buildings, but with seriously dwindling congregations. Members of HTB committed to move to these almost non-existent churches and subsequently the churches came alive again.

As curate of St Mark's I moved into a house on the edge of Clapham Common. I'd never had my own home before so it was a new experience for me. I had always shared accommodation with fellow students or work colleagues and consequently had virtually no furniture, although I had plenty of books. Setting up home was an exciting venture, however. The first piece of furniture I bought was a very substantial desk from the 1920s, which I still have sitting at home in my UK office.

ORDINATION

Besides settling in to my new home, I spent my time getting to know who was who in the church, and before long was heading off to the diocesan retreat house in preparation for my ordination.

The retreat house was in Bletchingley, Surrey. St Mary's, Bletchingley was the church where Archbishop Desmond Tutu famously served as a curate. I write this paragraph on the day that the great President Nelson Mandela died. I can never think of Archbishop Tutu without thinking of his great brother in reconciliation, Nelson Mandela. Looking back, it seems to me that the place of my final preparation for a life of ministry in reconciliation was no accident. It was the starting point for a great priest of reconciliation and it is utterly humbling to think that I began my service in the same place. Years later I would be honoured to spend time in the presence of both these great men.

The focus of the retreat was private prayer and I remember being inspired and uplifted by the words of the famous ordination hymn, "Veni, creator Spiritus".[5] After the retreat I travelled to Southwark Cathedral where the

---

5   Believed to have been written by Rabanus Maurus in the ninth century.

ordination itself would take place, carried out by the then Bishop of Southwark, Ronald Bowlby.

The fact that the ordination would take place at Southwark was also significant to me. It was here, at The Cathedral and Collegiate Church of St Saviour and St Mary Overie, to give it its full title, that the first British hospital was established in 1106 – my beloved St Thomas'.

Around a hundred of my friends came together for the event – former colleagues from St Thomas' and both Christian and Jewish friends from Cambridge. I was fairly certain that I was the only person being ordained that day who would have a kosher reception afterwards! The day sped by and, apart from the ordination ceremony itself, I most remember singing the old Charles Wesley hymn "Come, Holy Ghost, Our Hearts Inspire" and being flooded with God's presence. The Holy Ghost did indeed come that day and inspired me in a new way.

I returned home to Clapham for our kosher reception and everyone was so kind and encouraging. That evening I attended my first service at St Mark's as a member of the clergy and experienced the wonderful, genuine warmth of the congregation.

PARISH LIFE

My vicar, Paul Perkin, was obviously a man of substantial intellectual capacity. I soon noticed that all his sermons were immaculately prepared and presented. As well as being a respected Charismatic church leader, he was equally respected among the scholarly evangelical tradition, which had produced such great men as John Stott and Dick Lucas.

I felt very much the student again as I watched Paul go about his ministry with diligence and excellence, and I felt that I needed to aspire to his standard. I had much to learn in a short space of time, but Paul provided me with an outstanding grounding in ministry for which I will be forever grateful. I spent hours in sermon preparation, studying appropriate theological texts and commentaries. Frequently, I would become stuck and frustrated, and at these times I would phone my father in desperation. He was nearly always able to come to my aid.

I loved dealing with the pastoral needs of the congregation – visiting people, preparing for and taking funerals when necessary, and performing other parish duties. We had a diverse congregation that was split between the group of mainly young professionals who had moved from HTB and the local, predominantly working-class African-Caribbean community. But this apparent clash of cultures actually created a wonderful dynamic and I loved being at the church.

On my first night at St Mark's I met a man called Sergio who had come to the UK from Mozambique. It was clear to me that he had some mental health problems, but he had a great personality and I took a liking to him. Sergio was not depressed but schizophrenic and, at times, paranoid. I spent a great deal of time with him and often invited him round for meals.

Sergio was always reticent about telling me where he was living, but one day I persuaded him to show me where he was based. On arrival, I couldn't believe my eyes. He was in essence squatting in a derelict house. There was no water, no electricity, and very few floorboards – a complete hovel. It was also clear that Sergio had no means of supporting himself and received no help from anyone else, financial or otherwise. So that day I took him into my home to live with me.

I would like to say that he settled down at that point, but he didn't. One day I gave him some money to go out and buy food, and when he returned all he had bought were multiple boxes of bird seed. On another occasion I left Sergio alone in the house while I was away on an Alpha Course weekend, and when I returned I found that he had taken my front door off and put it back on the other way around. I eventually managed to persuade him to put it back how it was!

Lots of people thought I was mad to take someone like Sergio into my home, but God gave me such compassion for him that I had to do something – and this was just the beginning of people thinking that my actions were mad: there was more to come!

CAROLINE

I was involved in helping to organize a major mission in the parish that would host Britain's foremost evangelist, J. John. Previously I had heard him speak at a mission at Cambridge University and he was by far the most dynamic, entertaining, and funny speaker I'd ever heard, so I was looking forward to the mission and the plans were coming together well.

One night, as I was preaching at St Mark's, encouraging people to attend the mission and bring their friends, I noticed, sitting in the second row, the most beautiful young lady I'd ever seen. I thought to myself, "Wow! I like what I see," and I did! Immediately after the service I went over to greet her. We got chatting and I discovered that she was there with her sister. Caroline had previously been at St Helen's, Bishopsgate, in the City of London, and had just begun attending St Mark's with her sister, Sarah.

Caroline was a lawyer at one of the best firms in the City. I knew I wanted to see her again and so, being very spiritual about it, I asked if she and her sister would like to assist me with the mission planning. They agreed and later that week they both came round to my house.

By then I knew that I wanted Caroline to be more than just a fellow labourer in God's vineyard; I was falling in love with her and wanted to be with her all the time. But I had a rather large problem: I already had a girlfriend! I dealt with that matter as swiftly and kindly as I could and then, as soon as I could, I invited Caroline out to dinner. I was both relieved and thrilled when she agreed.

I took Caroline to the best restaurant on the edge of Clapham Common. I cannot remember a thing we had to eat; I just kept thinking how fortunate I was to be sitting opposite this beautiful person. After dinner we went for a walk on the Common under a moonlit sky and the atmosphere was just perfect. I stopped suddenly, looked into her eyes, and said, "Caroline, I think I love you." We hugged each other and then walked on, now holding hands. That was the beginning of my relationship with my beloved Caroline.

During the next few days we met almost every day and the following Sunday she invited me to her flat in Clapham for lunch. Caroline cooked us a fish pie. It was a memorable meal owing to the fact that fish pie is about the worst food I could ever be given, but I tried hard to be nice about it.

Our relationship flourished quickly. Caroline came along to a course I was leading at St Mark's called "Landmarks", which provided an excellent introduction to the basics of the

Christian faith. We had only been together for two weeks when I was invited to go to meet Caroline's family. Her parents lived on their family farm an hour outside London in a very affluent part of southern England. Their beautiful fifteenth-century farmhouse was stunning and the setting picturesque, with exquisite gardens and a full-size swimming pool. Also set inside the farm grounds was an ancient little chapel, which served the parish, since the village had a total of just five residences.

We spent a great weekend together and I had a wonderful time with Caroline's parents. I was delighted to see where Caroline had come from. Her father, Peter, was the senior partner in a very significant local law firm. He'd had a radical conversion to Christianity when Caroline was in her teens. He was filled to overflowing with the Holy Spirit and, at first, his family, who were all involved in the little village church, could not understand what had happened to him. Caroline's mother, Mary, was a full-time homemaker who frequently had bed and breakfast guests staying. They were both committed Christians who served the Lord through a variety of ministries. Peter was involved in the Full Gospel Business Men's Fellowship and would eventually become its UK president. He was also latterly an Anglican lay reader.

During the weekend we went to visit Caroline's grandmother in the next town. I noticed that she lived in a very nice, clean area. All the houses were large, detached properties and everything looked perfect. I commented to Caroline that I would hate to live in a place like this, where the streets were more like parks. I was happy living in downtown London. Years later, however, I find myself living not only on this very estate, but in the very house that belonged to Caroline's grandparents!

Wedding plans

When things became serious between Caroline and me, one of the first things I wanted to do was introduce her to my mentor, Lord Coggan, and his wife. It meant a lot to me that he would approve of her, which he clearly did. I therefore thought that I should waste no time in asking Caroline to marry me.

Since receiving my very first student grant, and from every subsequent pay cheque, I had taken the unusual step of putting aside some money for the day when I would need to buy an engagement ring. I set off for Hatton Garden, the renowned jewellery centre of London, to look for a ring and soon found exactly what I was looking for. As I left the jeweller's, in a very good mood, I was stopped on the street by the journalist and television presenter Esther Rantzen. She was making a programme about dancing and wanted to know if I was a dancing vicar. She managed to persuade me to dance down the street with one of the other presenters of *That's Life* and the clip featured in the opening credits of the show for a whole year. I became known as "the dancing vicar"!

I had not only planned ahead to save up for the engagement ring, but had also worked out exactly how I would propose when the time came. It was going to be while punting on the River Cam, between Clare College and King's College, Cambridge. I had been dating Caroline for less than a month, so it was extremely early in our relationship, but I knew without doubt that she was the one for me. I arranged the date and we went punting down the river on a perfect afternoon. Just after we had passed Clare College, I looked at her and said, "Caroline, will you marry me?" She looked up at me and said, "Maybe…" Still punting down the river, I said, "Please, my dear," and eventually she said, "Yes." I threw her the ring from where I was standing at the end of the punt.

The next day we visited her parents and I had the task of asking her father the big question: "May I marry your daughter?" Peter was a bit surprised. He said, "Well, I knew it would happen, but it is rather quick." I agreed with him that it was quick, but he had not said no, so I was nearly there, if not entirely!

Because I was a young cleric, I also needed to obtain permission from both my vicar and my bishop. Paul Perkin noted that Caroline had not been attending the church for very long, so he approved but with certain reservations. The bishop, however, approved totally and told me what he would say to my vicar, if he were in my position. I understood Paul's hesitation, though.

Meanwhile, while these events played out, we had the parish mission to carry out. I had heard J. John speak and now I was in the presence of the man himself. I introduced him to my dear Caroline and told him that we had got to know one another while planning for the mission. Little did I realize that, in due course, J. John and his wife, Killy, would become our closest friends. (Even this book has been written because J. John told me to get on with it!)

The mission was a great success and, once it was over, Caroline and I could begin planning our wedding. For me, the key thing was who would be the person to marry us. I dearly wanted it to be Lord Coggan, and I was delighted when he agreed. To preach we wanted David Armstrong from Holy Trinity, Cambridge. I had always had a strong belief in the ministry of the Word and Sacrament, so having the Word preached, followed by Holy Communion, was very important to us.

The wedding was due to take place at Caroline's family home, with the service held in the little chapel and the reception on the farm – all on the same site. The only slight problem with this arrangement was that the chapel was small and could hold only about 130 people. This obviously reduced the number of people who could attend and so we planned to have a second reception in London, after our honeymoon. We were filled with excitement as we looked forward to whatever adventures our new life together might bring.

CHAPTER 8

A New Life

Our impending marriage meant that I had a pressing matter to sort out. I still had Sergio living with me, and I could not put my new bride through the ordeal of living with a schizophrenic friend, so I had to set about getting professional psychiatric help for Sergio. For a while he was hospitalized to receive treatment; then social workers helped him to begin receiving regular benefit payments and also found him a nice apartment to live in. They even provided furniture for him. Sadly, Sergio's problems persisted, as did his odd behaviour. I went to visit him one day and saw a coffin sitting in the middle of his living room. I asked why it was there and Sergio told me that this was his bed, and that every morning when he woke up and got out of it he was born again. He went on to explain how he thought that most Christians had failed to realize that they needed to be born again every single day and that sleeping in a coffin was the way to achieve this.

Meanwhile, parish life continued and it was a joy to spend time in fellowship with many other colourful characters. Dr Charles Bartley was a consultant physician at St Thomas' and had also attended St Mark's, Kennington. He had been my teacher for a while. His deeply spiritual and dynamic wife, Madeline, led the church's prayer movement. Even though the relationship between Dr Bartley and me had changed now that I was no longer a medical student, I remained in awe of him.

Then there was an elderly Jamaican lady known as Sister Delilah Langley. She spoke in a wonderful deep, resonant voice with a strong West Indian accent and regularly cooked me rice, peas, and curried goat, which I loved. She had many wise sayings, such as, "Don't worry if you give God too much, because He will always give it back." It was a great quote, which I use to this day whenever I'm preaching on the subject of giving.

Friday was my day off and the day on which I pursued two passions from my former life. The first was that I would rise early and cycle to St Thomas' Hospital to work as a volunteer. This was not "normal" voluntary work, but working back in the operating theatre doing anaesthetics. I never did officially sign on with the hospital's volunteer bureau – I don't think they knew what to do with someone who wasn't there to make cups of tea or arrange flowers. It wasn't a "day off" as most people know it, but I thoroughly enjoyed keeping in contact with my old way of life.

The second was a continued involvement in Jewish–Christian relations. I was still chairing the young leadership section of the International Council of Christians and Jews. As a result, I regularly needed to travel to deal with various issues and, looking back, it must have seemed strange to the church members that their young curate was always whizzing around the world addressing international concerns, not least because I had developed a close relationship with Pope John Paul II and would, at times, pop over to the Vatican to see him. My relationship with the Pope had also developed out of my involvement in Jewish–Christian relations. When I was appointed chair of the young leadership section of the ICCJ, I also became part of the International Council's main board. Serving on the board was the senior bishop at the Holy See responsible for Jewish–Christian relations. He was taken with the radical development of our work and was convinced that the Holy Father would be interested in it. It was only a matter of weeks before I went to see him for the first time. By then I had just been ordained and was at the beginning of my curacy.

I had several invitations to go and see the Holy Father. It always seemed strange to me to be making regular trips to the Vatican and staying in a private part of the palace where all the cardinals stayed. On one occasion the Holy Father said he wanted to meet our entire young leadership group from around the world. I managed to raise sufficient funds to bring a delegation of young leaders from five continents, both Jews and Christians. I continued to see him until just before his death, when he was old and frail. I may have started by taking our young leaders group to meet him but I finished by introducing to him the Alexandria Declaration Group of chief rabbis, bishops, and imams. How it distressed me to see his physical decline: once we would go walking together in the gardens of the Vatican but by the end he could no longer even walk into his audiences. People have often asked me who are the greatest people I have ever met, and I always say the Catholic and the Protestant popes, John Paul II and Dr Billy Graham.

My curacy was fairly strange!

An unusual honeymoon

Lord Coggan was so helpful and strategic in the planning of our wedding. I recall his telling me very clearly that I was wrong in wanting to get married according to the 1662 Book of Common Prayer, which implied that marriage was mainly to do with overcoming the lusts of the flesh – at least, that is certainly what it implies. So Caroline and I allowed Lord Coggan to decide what service we would have, and what he chose was wonderful. It turned out that he wrote a lot of it himself.

We married on Easter Monday 1991. We had a great time and knew that the glory of the Lord was with us. Even though it was early spring, the weather could not have been better. One of my groomsmen, Bruce McKinnon, had been converted on the first Alpha Course I had ever led, and my best man was Richard Coombs, my great friend from Cambridge days who had chaired the controversial "Jews for Jesus" mission. At the wedding were also many Jewish friends from Cambridge, so the wedding itself was a symbol of reconciliation. At the reception there was kosher food on offer for all Orthodox Jewish guests.

Lord Coggan did a wonderful job, as did David Armstrong and Paul Perkin. The wedding reception was held in a grand marquee in the gardens right next to the chapel. Afterwards, according to tradition, the wedding guests were expecting a car to arrive to take us away for our honeymoon, but to everyone's surprise a helicopter appeared in the sky and landed to whisk us away for our first night in a country house before we left the next day for a trip abroad.

There was only one place we could go for our honeymoon as far as I was concerned, and that was to Israel – the place that had become so much more than my place of learning. It was my second home. I had decided that our first week together should be spent alone, so we went to the Golan Heights. It was an unusual honeymoon destination, I grant, given that it had been a war zone, but we spent our time up in the hills by rushing streams, overlooking the Sea of Galilee, and it was a wonderful, special place to begin our new life together.

From Galilee we headed up to Jerusalem. (Even though Jerusalem is south of Galilee you only "go up" to Jerusalem, so up we went!) We stayed in a very special place called Mishkenot Sha'ananim, which in Hebrew means "peaceful habitation". It was a row of almshouses built in 1860 by Sir Moses Montefiore, a British Jewish banker and philanthropist who worked for the establishment of a Jewish homeland. One could stay there only with the approval of the government or municipality. We had a wonderful time in Jerusalem meeting lots of my old friends and colleagues and going around seeing the wonderful sights of that great city.

We had one truly remarkable evening at the prestigious Yemen Moshe restaurant, next to where we were staying. We held a small reception there and a wide variety of my friends attended. I was amazed when my unnamed Hasidic rabbi friend turned up – as was everyone else. Moshe, the restaurant owner, came over to tell me that in twenty years no Hasidic person had ever set foot in his restaurant. It truly was a great honour and so humbling to have so many friends come together for such an important occasion.

One of my great friends who was there that day was Benji. Benji is the managing director of Regina Tours, one of the finest tour companies in Jerusalem. On the day we were married, Benji's wife, Zhava, had given birth to their daughter, Roni. Now, in Jerusalem, I got to hold baby Roni. I loved her from the moment I laid eyes on her and I love her just as much today. In fact, apart from Caroline and my own children I have never loved anyone as much as I do her. To this day, whenever I am in Jerusalem I have to see my Roni first. The agreement is that she is my Roni and I am her Andrew.

Roni has grown into the most beautiful young lady and is one of the most talented pianists I have ever heard. I digress to tell a story about her. As with most young ladies, the time came for her to fall in love. She found a wonderful young man called Omer, who is also a musician. Until I had met Omer I was as worried about Roni as if she were my own daughter. Was he good enough for her? Would he care for her properly? Would he truly love her? When I finally met him, however, there was no doubt that he was the right person and I loved him too. They became engaged and I knew without doubt that it was right.

I often listened to Roni playing the piano and recorded her on my phone. When Roni plays it brings the presence of God, and I would regularly listen to her music, particularly when things were difficult. A few years ago, I was kidnapped while I was in Iraq. I was searching for some people who had been kidnapped when I was captured myself. I was thrown into a very dark room and left alone. I could hardly see anything. Amazingly, my captors had not discovered and taken away my phone, so I used its light to survey my surroundings. Terrifyingly, I could see amputated fingers and toes strewn over the floor of my cell, so I immediately began to listen to Roni's music on my phone and focused on the presence of God. It is amazing how God always knows and gives us what we need. I immediately felt as though

I had been transported to heaven and I was later released without harm, calm and peaceful in the Lord's presence.

* * *

After our honeymoon, Caroline and I returned to Clapham. Whereas married life was great, I soon discovered that I was not the easiest person to live with! One of the more stupid things I did happened one evening when Caroline and I were preparing dinner. Caroline was chopping some carrots crossways and I told her that we wouldn't chop carrots like that in this house; we would cut them lengthways, that is the "proper" way. I soon discovered that this was not the kind of thing I should ever say. In fact, in every marriage preparation course I can think of, this (or something very like it) is cited as a typical example of the sort of thing one should *not* say!

This was not the only mistake I would make; there were many others. In fact, I am still making them, still learning, and probably will be for ever. The most important thing I have learned over the years, however, is always to remember kindness. Part of remembering kindness is realizing how unkind we can be, especially to those we love the most. It took me a little while to realize that I was married to a real saint. Every day of my life I see what incredible sacrifices Caroline makes in order to allow me to do what I do. She never ceases to amaze me.

A NEW CHURCH PLANT

It was not long into our first year of married life that Paul Perkin decided that St Mark's needed to plant out to another church. There were painstaking discussions about which parish the church ought to graft itself onto, and a church on the other side of Clapham was eventually identified.

I wondered who might be brought in to lead this new offshoot, since I was too young to be a vicar and had not finished serving my curacy. Other than that, I didn't think very much about the initiative. That was, until the bishop called me in to see him. He was keen that I should lead this new church. By now I had heard one or two other names mentioned, so I felt a bit caught in the middle of these discussions, but in due course it was decided that I should at least be interviewed for the position, and I agreed.

I was interviewed by the PCC – a lovely group of people – and it went very well. They had about fifty in their congregation and the idea was that I would bring around fifty people with me, some from St Mark's and some from HTB. So it was that at the tender age of twenty-eight I became the youngest vicar in the country – a priest in charge of my own parish.

When the news was announced, people from St Mark's began to volunteer to come with us and soon we had a very good team around us. We decided to call this a church "transplant" rather than a plant, recognizing the pre-existence of the church. It may have been small and struggling, but it was certainly still alive. So the day came when Caroline and I moved from our small terraced house to a very large house right opposite the new church in Clapham.

CHAPTER 9

Several Landmarks

The vicarage of the Church of the Ascension, Balham Hill, was like no other vicarage I had ever seen. At the front of the house there was a large sundial, embossed with the words, "Watch and Pray, Time Flies Away", and near the wall at the side of the house there stood a large statue of Jesus. The house was huge and I must confess that I loved it. It had four large reception rooms, six bedrooms, and four further rooms on the top floor, out of which had been created a self-contained apartment that had its own external staircase. All this space meant that I could have a fantastic study. I chose a lovely large room which was over thirty feet long and it was wonderful having a place where I could house my many books.

My installation at the church was a memorable event, with people present from the Church of the Ascension, St Mark's, and also HTB, who saw this church as one of their first "grandchildren" along with the Oak Tree Anglican Fellowship which had been planted out of St Barnabas, Kensington. During my first few weeks there the church grew as new members were added – not just those from the parent churches, but also some from St Mark's, Kennington.

As I have already mentioned, all the time I was a curate I spent my day off going back into St Thomas' to volunteer, and I continued to keep up this practice for a while. I worried at times that maybe I wasn't up to the job any more, but I was reassured by the number of consultants who continued to request my services. There were also a number of medical staff who required my presence at the hospital if they themselves needed to have surgery at some point, so occasionally I found myself back there during the week in a pastoral role, not just on my day off. I was able to do this now that I was in charge of my own parish.

The worship at the Church of the Ascension was wonderfully diverse. In the morning we would have a very traditional Anglican service and in the evening a more lively Charismatic service. All of the services were great and we witnessed the congregation grow considerably. This in itself was a wonderful sign of the validity and reality of various types of worship, working together in harmony.

I immersed myself in community life and got involved with every aspect of the parish. I became a governor of the local school and the chairman of the local community centre. I also got involved with other ministries in the parish, despite their not being Anglican. What bound us together was our commitment to the love and worship of God and a common desire to see our community come into a real relationship with the Almighty.

Another area of involvement was local politics. I had been interested in politics since my teens and had, at one time, been a member of the Young Conservatives. The parish of Balham Hill, in which the Church of the Ascension was located, was part of the London Borough of Wandsworth – the most Conservative borough in the country. I got to know many of the local councillors and party meetings would regularly be held in our home.

It was not long before I was asked if I would be prepared to stand for election as a councillor for the Balham ward. Neither did it take long for me to decide to say yes, though I was keenly aware that this decision would not be popular with all of my congregation.

It was very interesting canvassing for the election, because I knew a large number of the people I met. When the day eventually came for the vote, I remember wondering whether this really was something I should be doing, or not. I simply put the matter in God's hands and prayed, "Lord, if it is right, let me be elected. If not, then don't let me."

I went along to the count at the town hall that night and watched my pile of votes getting bigger and bigger. I was elected with a large majority. Later, when the party decided who should take on which role in the borough, I was surprised that I was immediately given the position of Deputy Chairman of Social Services. My particular responsibility was children's and young people's services, which encompassed such important issues as adoption and overseeing social workers for children. It was a big responsibility and one that brought with it major challenges.

I soon realized how complex politics is and the amount of compromises one has to make. I had studied politics, but being a practitioner was totally different. At meetings I found myself embroiled in debates, discussing the intricacies of borough life until late into the night. It was a steep learning curve. It was, however, useful training for the future. Whether I am dealing with politicians in the UK, the US, Iraq or Israel, I am always aware of the two main issues that occupy political minds: the compromises they will have to make and the people they need to keep happy.

Growth of international work

I continued my work for Jewish–Christian relations both in the UK and overseas with the International Council of Christians and Jews. Just as they had been at St Mark's, the parish council were a little surprised when I travelled abroad and met the Pope. But John Paul II was one of the finest people I had ever met and I loved spending time with him. I will never forget the occasion when I took Caroline with me to the Vatican. John Paul II looked quite shocked when I introduced her as my wife. Up to then, I don't think he had any idea that I was, in fact, an Anglican! He just knew that I was a young priest who was very involved in reconciliation between Jews and Christians. What variety of priest I was hadn't really mattered to him.

My parishioners were also beginning to realize that I was no normal parish priest. As well as my continuing involvement in Jewish–Christian relations, I was becoming more interested in the issue of persecuted Christians around the world. This meant a greater exposure to the Islamic world, particularly through a growing involvement with the Barnabas Fund, and I became one of their trustees. I was shocked by the immense suffering I began to see that was caused by religious intolerance, and it was not long before I began travelling to countries with a significant Muslim community – not just in the Middle East, but in African nations such as Kenya and Nigeria. I became particularly close to the Bishop of Kaduna, Josiah Idowu-Fearon, and stayed with him whenever I was in Nigeria. Although there was a Muslim majority in the nation, there was a significant Christian community, and it was a joy to join with them in worship. At the same time, there were major challenges regarding how to further the work of reconciliation in that nation.

Around this time I was approached by the Anglo-Israel Association to see if I was willing and able to lead a major delegation of church leaders to Israel. There would be a considerable budget allocated to the trip and I would have a lot of say in both the programme and the delegates. This seemed like far too good an opportunity to pass up, and I joyfully accepted it. The resulting delegation was very high-profile, including various senior bishops and other clergy. I shared the leadership of the tour with Lord Mackay of Clashfern, the former Lord Chancellor, and the Very Revd Dr James Harkness, the former Moderator of the Church of Scotland.

As well as enabling me to engage once again with many of the people I had grown to love in the Holy Land, this trip gave me the opportunity to connect with Israel at the highest level, from the president down. Back in London, I began to engage with both the British and Israeli governments on issues relating to Israel and the Palestinian Authority. Rather than treat this as something separate from my life as a parish priest, I sought to involve the people of the Church of the Ascension in what I was doing. On several occasions we had both Jewish and Christian delegations visit us from over thirty different countries. Bishops from Kenya came and Bishop Josiah from Nigeria was a regular visitor.

Despite my growing international focus, however, my parish had to be my first priority. I travelled around it on my bicycle so that I could stop and engage with whoever happened to be out on the streets. The local community was part and parcel of my daily life and most days I would have lunch with the senior citizens who frequented the local community centre.

A new arrival

In 1996, halfway through our time at Balham Hill, Caroline became pregnant. As far as I was concerned, there was no place she could be cared for other than St Thomas', and by my favourite obstetrician and friend Ian Fergusson – the surgeon who liked me for my big hands! Caroline and I went to see him together and he looked after her wonderfully.

The pregnancy went well and the day came when Caroline went into labour. Our good friend Laura Wallace, who lived two doors down, took Caroline to the hospital and I followed shortly after. On approaching the labour ward I spotted one of the consultant anaesthetists I had worked with, Dr Tessa Hunt. She was one of the top obstetric anaesthetists in the country. We had already decided that Caroline would have an epidural during the birth and so Tessa decided to accompany me to the ward and duly instructed me to set up for the epidural. It was just as if I were back in my old role! Tessa performed the epidural herself and though Caroline had a long, hard labour there was no pain, as the doctor had done an excellent job as usual.

Eventually our child was born and we named him Josiah Peter Bartholomew. In just a few weeks he would be baptized by the same person who had married Caroline and me, Donald, Lord Coggan. There we were with our Josiah in St Thomas' Hospital, overlooking the Thames, the Houses of Parliament, and the hospital gardens, the very place I'd been standing when God had called me to leave medicine and go to Cambridge to study theology. As I write this now, it is Josiah who is a student at Cambridge. I will never forget trying to persuade Josiah, whom I always call Yossi, to study

Hebrew or Arabic. He told me clearly, "Daddy, you're from the past; I'm from the future. I'm doing Chinese!"

A tragedy

A year later, into the midst of this happy, buzzing life came some tragic news. My brother, Mark, had been very unwell for a number of years and he had given up going to see the doctors at his local hospital because they had never been able to do anything for him. He still lived at home with my parents, but he hardly ever left the house and spent most of his time in bed. Then one day he suddenly went out, not telling my parents why or where he was going. He didn't return that evening as expected. My parents were extremely worried and next morning we informed the police. It wasn't easy convincing them that there was something serious about a young man in his twenties with a nondescript illness going missing for one night.

Two more nights passed and I awoke to the news of the tragic death of Diana, Princess of Wales. It was a Sunday morning and I had members of her family in our congregation. After the morning service we had a special service dedicated to her memory. It was an incredibly moving experience. While this special service was still under way, two policemen came into the church and indicated that they needed to speak with me. I waited until the next hymn began and then went over to talk to them. The news was not good. My dear brother's body had been found, washed up on the shore at Dover.

I returned to the podium and had to continue the service. At the very end, after the blessing, I told the congregation of the devastating news I had just received. People could not believe I had managed to continue with the service despite this tragic event. I asked our precious people to pray with me, and then I had the task of going to visit my parents to share this terrible news with them.

Mark had been ill for a long time, but, nevertheless, when tragedy strikes it hurts so much and nothing can prepare you for this kind of emotional agony. I arrived at my parents' house and broke the news. I remember nothing of the event apart from all our tears and pain. The next few days were a blur, spent organizing his funeral. I wanted to take Mark's funeral service myself, even though I was worried that I would not make it to the end. But I was thankful to the Lord that He got me through it and the church was packed with our congregation and many of my friends, for which I was truly grateful.

CHAPTER 10

Sent to Coventry

Sitting in my study in Balham one day, I received a phone call, after which everything in my life changed. It was my diocesan bishop, Roy Williamson, a wonderful man whom I was honoured to serve under. We often chatted on the phone, but this conversation was very different. He told me he wanted to send me to Coventry. For international readers, this phrase has a double meaning in the UK, where "to send someone to Coventry" means to ostracize them and generally pretend that they don't exist! But Bishop Roy wanted me to apply for a highly significant and very senior role in the Church of England.

It was the position of Residentiary Canon of Coventry Cathedral, also working as Director of International Ministry and Director of the International Centre for Reconciliation. There was, however, no guarantee that I would be appointed, since it was such a senior role in the church and I was still relatively junior. It would also require a long selection procedure. Yet I felt that God was directing me to apply and it sounded so much in line with my growing involvement in reconciliation work. While filling in the numerous forms and updating my CV, I was struck by just how much diverse experience I had gained in the area of reconciliation.

I arrived in Coventry the day before my interview so that I could look round the cathedral and attend a service there. I found it a very moving experience. I had read much of the story of the destruction and rebuilding of Coventry Cathedral, but seeing it first-hand was totally different. The bombed-out ruins of the old cathedral standing side by side with the new, modern one formed a wonderful picture of death and resurrection.

It was the first service I'd experienced in a cathedral, worshipping with many other people. As the choir processed it was like hearing the singing of angels. I didn't know a great deal about the complexities of the job I was applying for, but I did know that I wanted to be here in this wonderful place. The opportunity to have a job in international reconciliation, at the same time rooted in the church, seemed too good to be true. I sat in awe in the cathedral, thinking about my interview the next day.

On the Monday morning I returned to the cathedral to face a large, impressive panel of people. I didn't know any of them, but they all seemed to be very high-powered individuals. The panel was led by the then Bishop of Coventry, Colin Bennetts, and the equally impressive Provost, John Petty. They questioned me long and hard! They seemed to be rather amazed that, at such a young age, I had acquired such a wealth of international experience. I mentioned to them that I had only really become aware of the breadth and depth of my experience as I had been completing the application form. The interview seemed to go as well as could be expected, and then I had to rush back to London to attend a Wandsworth Council election.

I was at something of a crossroads in my life. My interview in Coventry had dovetailed together with a vote for re-election to Wandsworth Council. Once again I put the matter in the Lord's hands.

"Lord," I prayed, "I want to be either re-elected or given the job in Coventry, but not both." Once again I saw my pile of votes getting bigger and eventually I was elected again with a large majority. With some disappointment I thought to myself, "OK, maybe I *am* supposed to stay here, then." I had had an amazing time in Coventry and it seemed like my dream job, but God knew best.

The next morning, however, Bishop Colin Bennetts called me from Coventry. He told me that the selection committee had unanimously decided that they wanted to appoint me as Canon Director of International Ministry and Director of the International Centre for Reconciliation. I was surprised, after having been re-elected in London, but clearly God had other plans. I assured the bishop that I would be honoured and delighted to accept the position.

There remained just one minor obstacle to my taking up this appointment. Officially, I was too young! The post of Residentiary Canon required one to be at least thirty-three years old. I was still thirty-two and my birthday was several months away, so I had some time to wait before I could be installed in this new position.

So much had happened in such a short time. I had a new position on my local council and a new job miles away in the Midlands. My agreement with the bishop was that I would not make any announcement regarding my appointment until the date had been set for my installation at Coventry Cathedral. The conversation at church the following Sunday therefore revolved around my re-election to Wandsworth

Council. I realized the gravity of taking on such a role. If there were any problems with the borough's social services, it would be my fault and my responsibility to sort them out. I accepted this and was sure that I would do everything possible to ensure any issues were dealt with.

For a short while parish life continued as normal, but with the added responsibility of running backwards and forwards to meetings in a variety of social services departments to discuss many different concerns.

Eventually I received news from the bishop regarding my installation at Coventry Cathedral. It meant that at last I could tell my dear congregation that I would be leaving them. When that moment came, it was much harder and more painful than I had anticipated. I had truly grown to love these people. I had seen the church grow to several hundred and I was involved in every aspect of parish life. As I broke the news, I burst into tears. To my total surprise, many of the congregation began to cry as well. I knew then, if not before, just how tight-knit a community we had become, living and worshipping together. The one consolation I had was that, although I would no longer be their vicar, I would still be their councillor. Exactly how the latter was going to work, with my being based in Coventry, I didn't really know.

Of course, there was one other implication of the move to Coventry to take up a demanding new role. It meant that my days off would no longer be spent volunteering at my beloved St Thomas' Hospital. On my last day there I said my goodbyes and left the hospital with a parting souvenir: my custom-made, size-sixteen, operating-theatre Wellington boots. I knew that this part of my life had finally come to an end.

Caroline was pregnant with our second child as we packed up our belongings and prepared to move to Coventry. It was hard work for both of us, but at the same time we were filled with eager anticipation about moving to a new place and settling in. Coventry would prove to be a shock to the system – a totally different social environment from anything we had known previously – but we greeted it with much excitement.

The day finally came for my installation at Coventry Cathedral and I was deeply touched by the fact that hundreds of people made the effort to travel up from London for the event. Most of the church came in coaches, along with many members of Wandsworth Council, including the then mayor. It was a truly grand event and, looking back on it now, it marked the beginning of a completely different way of life for me – one in which I would never again be permanently based in the UK.

The very day after my installation, work began in earnest. I clearly had a huge amount to learn. My predecessor was the very well-known, left-wing Canon Paul Oestreicher, and here was I, a right-wing Tory councillor taking over his role. Paul was still based in Coventry and, despite our marked political differences, we got on very well. The fact that he was still around to consult meant that I could learn much from him, not least about Coventry's long historical involvement in reconciliation and its worldwide community, the Cross of Nails. This organization, which worked for reconciliation, had taken its name from Coventry's famous symbol of reconciliation – a cross wrought from three large nails that fell from the roof of the cathedral when it was bombed on 14 November 1940. Around the world, many places committed to reconciliation had become partners with Cross of Nails in the search for peace.

Parallel to my steep learning curve in the field of international reconciliation ran learning about the role and responsibilities of a cathedral canon. Being a canon had no similarities with being in a large parish church at all. Instead of sharing in the worship, I was now leading it, accompanied by the most exquisite choir. Besides that, there were many other different tasks that needed to be accomplished. I had, however, invited two of my most significant staff from London to move with me to Coventry and thankfully they had accepted, so we were already forming a good team.

From the beginning it was not easy to juggle my diverse responsibilities. I needed to travel down to London by train regularly on a Saturday morning to participate in council surgeries and also late at night during the week for council meetings. Aside from all the travel, my new council role presented me with great challenges. At one time I was forced to make some cuts in the social services budget, which was a highly unpopular move. Shortly after I arrived at the town hall one day, I was faced with a huge crowd of protestors baying for my blood. They were chanting, "Fire the Canon!" and had banners proclaiming "Cut church services not social services". I must admit that I went over to the protestors and told them how good I thought their slogans were!

FURTHER HEALTH CHALLENGES

As I settled into my role, it was clear that the scope of my ministry and calling would be different from the work that had gone on before. It was not going to be just a continuation of the involvement in the traditional places of Coventry's reconciliation efforts. God had called me to, and given me a special understanding of, the Middle East, so I was keen to expand the ministry in that direction.

I had not been at Coventry long, however, and had not made even a single overseas trip when I started having problems with my balance. Shortly after this began, I started losing some vision in my right eye. I went to see a local doctor and he referred me immediately to a neurologist.

The consultant neurologist was a very nice man who happened to be a Nigerian Muslim. The fact that I had spent a lot of time visiting Muslim areas of Nigeria was of considerable interest to him. He was obviously very concerned about my symptoms and said he wanted to admit me to hospital straight away for further tests. I took up residence on the neurological ward of the Walsgrave Hospital in Coventry. By now I was developing other symptoms and beginning to feel very ill.

A large number of tests followed, and the consultant made it clear to me that the symptoms could be very serious, pointing as they did to a condition such as multiple sclerosis. During my time at St Thomas' Hospital my one non-surgical allocation had been to the neurology department, so I did know a little about the subject. My stay in hospital proved to be longer than I had expected. I had been in there four weeks when they decided I needed a lumbar puncture to test my cerebral spinal fluid. I knew that this test could be definitive in the diagnosis of MS.

By this time Caroline was due to deliver our second child and she was scheduled to be in another hospital. I desperately wanted to be at the birth and we managed to get the location of delivery transferred to the same hospital that I was in. I had my lumbar puncture and felt very unwell afterwards, with the expected excruciating headaches and an inability to sit upright. It was all rather tough, but I knew it had to happen.

Just a few days after this Caroline went into labour and I received the news that she would shortly be on her way to the hospital. At the same time the neurology consultant was doing his ward round and I saw him making his way over to me. I could tell from the look on his face that he didn't have good news for me. He told me that they had found oligoclonal immunoglobulin bands in my cerebral spinal fluid. It was a conclusive sign that I did, in fact, have MS. I phoned Caroline, who had not yet left for the hospital, and told her my news, shedding many tears in the process. But my dear wife was in labour and about to come to the hospital herself, so I quickly changed my mindset from that of a patient to that of a husband whose wife was about to give birth.

I phoned John Petty, the provost at the cathedral, to tell him about my diagnosis. As ever, he spoke positively about the power of prayer for healing and was very reassuring.

Shortly after this, Caroline arrived on the labour ward and I was taken in a wheelchair to see her. She was doing very well, considering that she was about to give birth and she'd just been told that her husband had been diagnosed with an incurable disease.

In due course, a substantial ten-pound baby appeared, another boy. We had decided on the name Aaron, which pleased me as it reminded me of Rebbe Aaron the Great of Karlin, founder of the Karlin-Stolin Hasidic Jewish movement. The next day our elder son, Josiah, aged two and a half, came to the hospital to see me, his mummy, and the new baby. Josiah, though young, was so emotional about seeing Aaron that he called him his new sister. We assured him that Aaron was his brother, not his sister, but for a while he remained unconvinced, certain that he had a sister!

Two days later Caroline left hospital and I was allowed out 'the following weekend. Caroline and I had a big conversation about Aaron's name. In the end we both decided that we should change it to Jacob. I was pleased about this too, however, because Jacob/Jacobus was the name of the current Karliner Rebbe, who had influenced me very much when I was a student in Jerusalem. So Jacob it was. Josiah then had to come to terms with the fact that his sibling was a brother and not a sister, and that he was in fact called Jacob and not Aaron! Getting hold of this concept took a while, but eventually Josiah was happy with it.

Despite my diagnosis I was very soon back at work in the cathedral and even back on my pushbike. I was now planning my first overseas trip, which would be to Israel. This would turn out to be a good trip, during which I would be able to renew links with many of my old colleagues. Later that year I was also able to visit many of the centres with which Coventry had long-standing links, both in Germany and across America.

The next major change in my work and life would come in December 1998. Operation Desert Fox saw a combined US and UK military attack on Iraq with a major four-day bombing campaign from 16–19 December, designed to stem the rise of Saddam Hussein's military power. During those four days, much of Iraq was decimated. I was totally shocked by this radical military attack, knowing how it would affect the lives of ordinary people. I made my feelings known publicly to the media and our own government.

At the time Britain had no official diplomatic relationship with Iraq and therefore did not have an Iraqi embassy or ambassador. The only link was an Iraqi interest section at the Jordanian Embassy, the head of which had become a friend of mine. I decided that I wanted to travel to Iraq to see if there was anything I could do to try to establish a relationship between Britain and Iraq. It was not, however, easy to get an invitation to visit Iraq. Every attempt I made failed and I was told emphatically, "We don't want you here. Just stop bombing us." It was hard to communicate the fact that it wasn't me personally who was doing the bombing.

In the end, I gathered my team together and we prayed about the matter. The very next day I was contacted with an invitation from Saddam Hussein's deputy, Tariq Aziz, to visit Iraq. After trying many different ways to try to get into Iraq, I had finally turned to prayer. That day I learned a very big lesson about how to conduct my work. Though I might try to use the routes of politics and diplomacy to get where I wanted, in the end, where I went and what I did was up to God. He was in charge, not me.

CHAPTER 11

To the Middle East

Following the miraculous provision of an invitation to visit Iraq, I began to prepare for the trip. I was surprised by the amount of interest shown by the national media in my going there. The BBC gave me a recorder to take with me so that I could make an in-depth radio programme. Many radio and TV interviews followed, such was the fascination with why a cleric had decided to visit what was probably the most dangerous country in the world for a Westerner at that time.

I arrived in Jordan and spent the night in Amman before setting off for Iraq at 4.30 the next morning. In those days there were no flights into the country, as they had been banned under radical international sanctions, so the only route in was via a very long drive, which I was not particularly looking forward to. I had with me a British Iraqi called Riad, who would be my driver. We set off and drove for some six hours to get to the Iraqi border. This was followed by a tortuous three-hour visa transfer process before we could be allowed into the country. The small border reception office was filthy. It had no phone connection, certainly no Internet access, and there appeared to be very little organization. It was like entering another world. Eventually we were allowed into Iraq to begin the second leg of our journey.

The first thing that one noticed about Iraq was the state of the vehicles at the sides of the roads as we travelled away from the border. The vast majority of them had broken windows and many looked as if they would never run again. It was the first sign of the effect that the UN sanctions were having on the nation. After that we were faced with many hours of driving through nothing but flat, faceless desert. There was nothing of interest to look at until we got closer to Baghdad. There we saw the towns of Ramadi and Fallujah. Little did I know how significant those places would become in years to come.

Fifteen hours after leaving Jordan we arrived at a hotel in Baghdad that I would frequent regularly over the years. The Al Rasheed Hotel was owned by the Iraqi government. As you entered the foyer you couldn't fail to notice the marble floor, which had a huge mosaic of George Bush Senior embedded in it, proclaiming "Bush is criminal" in both English and Arabic. Upon arrival I was met by a delegation from the "Ministry of Protocol". I had never heard of this particular government department and felt convinced that they were Mukhabarat – the Iraqi secret police. In other words, spies who would be watching my every move and listening to every word. When I got to my room there was a Mukhabarat officer sitting outside, where he would remain around the clock. I presumed that my room was also bugged and there was evidence to support this. It was my first, uncomfortable, experience of being continually watched.

Breakfast the next morning was awful, consisting of some stale bread and grim-tasting tea. It was beginning to dawn on me that everything here was awful. Then it was time for another meeting with the people from the Ministry of Protocol to discuss my programme for the trip. It was made abundantly clear to me that there was no flexibility whatsoever in my schedule – everything I would do had already been decided on by the government. I would be visiting various ministries in the nation, but would begin by seeing a bombed air-raid shelter which had been attacked in the war of 1991. I was informed that this was to happen immediately, so within minutes I was on my way.

THE REALITY OF CONFLICT

What I was faced with when I arrived was quite unbelievable. On the walls of the shelter, which had been horrendously bombed, were pictures of everyone who had been killed. A lady showed me around and she paused in front of a picture of a group of ten children. They were all her children. She explained that the only reason she herself was alive was that she had risked her life to go out to find food for her children. The bombs had hit while she was gone.

This was heartbreaking, but one image will remain with me for ever. In the shelter there had been a lady standing up, holding her baby, when a bomb struck. The blast had etched her outline onto the shelter wall as it killed her and her child. This place was horrendous. Even here, at the beginning of my trip, it was clear to see that such tragic effects of the conflict were being used as propaganda.

The meetings that followed were with political and religious leaders. Each person had the same message: the serious effect that international sanctions were having on Iraq as a whole. Then I was taken to see the state of their hospitals, all of which were in serious disrepair. What was of particular concern was the number of children who were suffering from illnesses such as leukaemia and terrible congenital deformities. I was told that all these conditions were the result of the radioactive depleted uranium that covered many of the missiles dropped on the nation during the 1991 war. Sadly, research by many had confirmed that this was indeed the case. Through all of this I became convinced that a major priority of mine must be the fighting of sanctions and objecting to the use of radioactive materials in weapons.

Eventually, I was taken to a palace to meet Tariq Aziz – a man clearly revered by those who were watching and escorting me. In a short while I found myself in the presence of the man I had seen so many times on television. In that meeting I heard a repetition of the story I had been hearing over and over: how the sanctions were affecting the entire nation, and how the dispersal of depleted uranium had caused a massive health crisis. I was beginning to see that central to any reconciliation work was going to be the skill of building good relationships with people whose ideology was diametrically opposed to my own.

By culture, Aziz was considered a Christian, but I was convinced that no one could work so closely with Saddam Hussein for so many years without being affected by him. Our meeting got off to a good start, however, and I was hopeful that we could form a good relationship. Aziz could tell that I truly cared about his nation and the plight of ordinary Iraqis, and he told me that I was welcome to come back and visit at any time.

Before I left he asked me if there was any way that I could come back and bring a delegation of church leaders with me, so that they too could see what the situation was really like. I assured him that I would try my best to arrange this.

I was beginning to get a glimpse of what it was that I could do regarding Iraq.

Fifteen years on I am typing this on my laptop in the back of a car driving through Baghdad. I am on my way to see Tariq Aziz again, not in his palace but in his prison cell. He is now an old man on death row.[6] Oh, how people's stories change.

There was one other memorable visit on this first trip – to the home of the Sisters of Charity. The Mother Teresa Sisters had established a wonderful home to care for children born after the war with major congenital deformities. I was so impressed by what these wonderful ladies were doing to look after these most vulnerable and needy little ones. I wanted to take some pictures, but I was told it was forbidden. I wondered why and was informed that they were concerned that others might use the pictures for fundraising efforts for the home. I thought this strange: wouldn't they want people to raise funds to keep the charity going? But one of the sisters told me, "God was great enough and big enough to make the whole world, so He can certainly make sure we have what we need to survive." I learned so much from them about relying on our Father to meet all our needs according to His riches in glory.

To this day the home is still there and I visit it every week when I am in Iraq, to see the children and the sisters, who have become dear friends. Fifteen years after my first visit it is an important part of my life. The children who are cared for there are still those who, in the main, have been abandoned to die, often without limbs, or with other major congenital problems.

---

6   See Afterword.

I had one last visit to make in Iraq before the end of my trip, and that was to the single Anglican church in Baghdad, on Haifa Street. The church had been closed down and deregistered by the Iraqi government after the bombing by the US and UK in 1991. The congregation had been made up of expatriates. Now it was totally devoid of any community.

A caretaker, Hanna, had recently been appointed to look after the building by the Bishop of Cyprus and the Gulf, Clive Handford. Iraq was in his diocese, even though there was no functioning Anglican Church there. Hanna took me inside. The building was utterly derelict and filthy. Since it had not been a functioning church for about fourteen years, the building had been totally looted and not a single pew remained. Many of the windows had been broken, the organ had been removed, and the only church fixture that remained was the solid marble font. The only sign of life there were the pigeons that lived inside the building.

I was dismayed that the church should be in such a terrible condition. Despite having a caretaker, it was not being cared for at all. I gave Hanna very clear instructions on how the place should be looked after. I made it plain that I would be back soon and that I would expect the church by then to be clean, tidy, and in a good state. I was assured it would be. I remember praying to God that one day the church would be alive and functioning again. I never dreamed that one day this would by *my* church; that it would become one of the largest, most vibrant churches in Iraq and the entire congregation would be Iraqi.

Growing links with Palestine

My driver, Riad, and I left to embark on the long drive back across the Iraqi border and into Jordan. I felt determined to begin this new process of relationship building and reconciliation work in Iraq. I would return here soon. Meanwhile, I had to complete my work on the radio programme for the BBC. In due course it was broadcast and received a very positive response. Coventry was seen as the City of Peace and now its man of peace had visited Iraq. Following on from this, I had a discussion with my bishop, Colin Bennetts, and others about the prospect of taking a delegation of church leaders out to Iraq. They all agreed it would be a good idea and were excited about the project.

In the meantime, I needed to visit Israel and Palestine to take forward the work I'd already begun there. Initially, my relationships had been mainly with the Jewish community, but increasingly I was forming links with the Palestinian community at every level. Some of these connections were especially politically significant. One such person was Imil Jarjoui, the owner of the Christmas Hotel in East Jerusalem. Dr Jarjoui would later be elected as a member of the Palestinian Legislative Council and the PLO Executive Committee. He was a key political player. As we talked about various peacemaking initiatives he told me unequivocally that one thing I must do, if I wanted to make any progress, was to go and meet President Yasser Arafat.

This, I must say, did not really please me. Having spent so much time with the Israelis for so long, I was not particularly favourable towards Arafat. I took Dr Jarjoui's advice, however, and asked to meet him. When this eventually happened, we had a long and positive meeting. While I was there I was reminded again that the task of reconciliation and peacemaking means meeting and forming relationships with those who are not your friends and may even be your enemies. But reconciliation is about how we apply grace in the midst of conflict for the sake of a greater cause.

This was the first of many meetings between me and Yasser Arafat. For years afterwards I would go and see him in Ramallah on the West Bank every time I visited Israel. We grew to be very good friends and remained close until his death in 2004. Through him I discovered what it was to love a person who, ideologically, was opposed to everything one believed in.

At the same time as developing connections with the Palestinians, I maintained close relationships with my Israeli Jewish friends and colleagues. This was the cause of some controversy. Interestingly, the people who were complaining about my befriending the Palestinians were not Israeli Jews, but pro-Israel Western Christians. Similarly, it was pro-Palestine Western Christians who were offended by my befriending Israeli Jews. I realized for the first time that perhaps Christians in the West were another facet of the problem, as they were adding to the division rather than the reconciliation efforts. To this day I still say that what we must do is work towards loving both sets of people, Israeli and Palestinian alike.

CHAPTER 12

Return to Iraq

I had made progress with my plans to return to Iraq and had assembled a number of delegates for the trip. Along with me there would be my bishop, Colin Bennetts, and Peter Price, my former bishop in Kingston, responsible for much of south London. We had also arranged to take Clive Handford, Bishop of Cyprus and the Gulf, and the final member was Patrick Sookhdeo, then Director of the Barnabas Fund, whose main work was to support those in the suffering church.

We flew to Jordan and then began the long drive across the desert, the same boring route I'd travelled previously. This was to be the first of many such long journeys I would make with Bishop Colin, but I soon learned that they were a gift from God. Very few people ever have the opportunity to spend several hours with their bishop and Bishop Colin was a remarkable man. I loved him and grew to enjoy the arduous drive across the desert.

We arrived in Baghdad and checked into the same dirty hotel with its warning about George Bush Sr. We were even greeted by the same spies as last time and told that in the morning we would have a similar briefing regarding our itinerary for the trip.

The next morning our programme was explained to us. As before, precisely when things would happen we would not know. The only certainty was that we would go first to the terrible air-raid shelter, before undertaking various meetings with political and religious leaders. Eventually, at some point, we would also meet Tariq Aziz.

Our delegation heard exactly the same stories that I had on my initial visit – of the suffering caused by sanctions and the physical effects that depleted uranium had had on the population. During these discussions, it began to dawn on me just how scared everyone was. People were afraid to speak freely about anything, for fear of reprisals from Saddam. Even when we sat down to talk with religious leaders, it was obvious that they were being scrutinized by our spies. Every word they said was written down and, if necessary, could be used against them later.

During our trip, Bishop Colin asked if it would be possible to visit a particular family he knew. Previously he had been the vicar of St Andrew's, Oxford and during his time there some Iraqis who were studying at the university had attended the church. Our minders duly granted this request and we got to meet this wonderful family. Hermes Hanna was a retired headmaster and his wife, Maria, a retired headmistress. They had a son, Gehad, who was a flight lieutenant in the Iraqi air force. After this initial meeting I would see Gehad on every subsequent visit to Iraq, and fifteen years later he is a fluent English speaker and a member of my staff in England. Eventually, after the 2003 war, he and his family were forced to flee Iraq because they were threatened over their links with the West. It may have seemed awful at the time, but we are grateful for God's protection and that this precious family are still with us.

Our trip continued and eventually we saw Tariq Aziz. It was a good meeting and at the end he made it clear that he wanted our relationship with Iraq to continue and become a long-term arrangement.

Before leaving Iraq we visited St George's Church. Hanna, the caretaker, had cleaned up the building as I had asked, and Bishop Clive celebrated Holy Communion there for us.

One final significant event occurred before we left to return home. I was introduced to a man who was a lay reader at a Presbyterian church in Baghdad. He was a retired air vice-marshal – having basically run the Iraqi air force – and his name was General Georges Sada. In time he would become my right-hand man in Iraq and be an immeasurable help to my work there. After the 2003 war he became famous for writing the book *Saddam's Secrets*,[7] in which he showed that Saddam did indeed possess chemical weapons, which he moved to Syria before the war.

* * *

On each subsequent visit to Iraq I built stronger relationships with various political and community leaders. As trust grew between me and the security services I was able to have more say in what I did, but I was never totally free of the secret-police spies and never had the freedom to go around or do anything on my own. Georges Sada now accompanied me wherever I went, however, which made things considerably easier.

Each visit included a meeting with Tariq Aziz. On one occasion he said to me, "You have brought your religious

---

7   Published by Thomas Nelson, 2009.

leaders here to Iraq; can you now take ours to England and America?" I told him that I could certainly host an Iraqi religious delegation in the UK, but the US was a different matter.

"I don't know anyone who can make that happen," I told him. He simply turned to me and said, "Ask Billy Graham." This surprised me, but I went away and did exactly what he suggested. I certainly thought that it would help relations if I were to accompany a group of Iraqi religious leaders on trips to the UK and the US, so I began making plans for it to take place. The English side was easy enough and I contacted the office of Dr Billy Graham for assistance with the US side of things. It so happened that Iraq was one of his great concerns, and he was happy to help.

After much logistical work and planning we had a good programme organized for both the UK and the US. It would begin in the States with a meeting with Dr Graham himself. The Iraqi government had selected three of its most senior religious leaders to make up its delegation. Ayatollah Hussein Al-Sadr was a Grand Ayatollah from Baghdad and one of the key Shia leaders in Iraq. Then there was a senior Sunni, Sheikh Dr Abdul Latif Humayeem, who was not only the most senior Sunni sheikh but also the personal imam of Saddam Hussein. The final member was the Patriarch of the Chaldean Catholic Church, Raphael Bidawid.

The trip began with my flying to New York where I was to rendezvous with the Iraqi delegation before taking them to see Dr Graham. I found myself waiting at the airport for hours, eagerly watching flights arriving, but there was no sign of them. Eventually I received a phone call saying that they were all stuck in Jordan. They had planned to travel to America with a Jordanian airline, but the US had made it clear that, if they did, they would not be allowed entry into the country when they arrived. Even though I was certain we had obtained security clearance for them at every point of their journey, it didn't seem to be working. I then heard the rumour that the trip was being blocked by the CIA.

Eventually, I had to concede that I would be going to see Dr Billy Graham on my own. We had a wonderful meeting. I had met many high-profile people in my life so far, from archbishops to heads of state, but I had never met anyone like Dr Graham. He was a statesman of the church and had an incredible warmth and godly presence about him. To this day I have only ever met two people like this, whose very presence has an immediate effect upon one: Dr Graham and Pope John Paul II.

We talked at length about my work in Iraq. In those early days the ministry looked very different from how it looks today. We had no functioning church, no medical clinic, no school or relief programme – I was just working flat out trying to lay the foundations of reconciliation and deal with the effects of sanctions.

We soon got talking about what to do with the Iraqi delegation. Dr Graham had a very wise assistant, Dr John Ackers, who commented that it was clear we had done everything we possibly could and nothing had worked; therefore, the only thing we could do was to ask Dr Graham to call the president, Bill Clinton. At that time, Mr Clinton's affair with Monica Lewinsky had just been uncovered by the media. Dr Graham was reluctant to get in touch with him during this sensitive time, but he could also see that no other course of action would yield the desired result, so he called Bill Clinton and the process of getting the Iraqi leaders into the US had a sudden kick start. But even then it was not without its complications. The delegation had to endure a huge number of security procedures and owing to Dr Graham's schedule we had to move the location of the meeting from New York to Boston.

The meeting took place and we spent a very valuable time together. Afterwards there followed a series of meetings with many different politicians and representatives of the United Nations. After a few days we flew to the UK to begin the second part of the trip.

The whole venture was an intensive learning process for me. I had no real understanding of the expectations of Middle Eastern religious leaders when it came to accommodation. Basically, I thought that during their stay we could provide for them in the same way that we would have provided for fellow British church leaders. For instance, we began the trip in Coventry, an industrial town in the Midlands. The city did not possess a Grand Hotel, so we had arranged a nice, clean, simple three-star hotel. It quickly became apparent that this was far from acceptable, but the fact was, there was nowhere better to stay – and it was certainly much better than the accommodation I'd had in Baghdad.

Nevertheless, we had a very good series of meetings in Coventry, based at the cathedral. After this we moved to London, where we'd arranged to stay in a very nice retreat house. Again, it was made clear that these men were not looking for functional comfort but for luxury, so at great expense we had to move them to a large, opulent hotel in central London while I boarded at a monastery! Finally our guests were happy and we could continue with our programme.

Just as on the US leg of our trip, our meetings were varied and diverse and included speaking to gatherings

of both religious and political leaders. One of our main
meetings was at Chatham House, otherwise known at the
Royal Institute of International Affairs. The audience were
very powerful people and included many diplomats. But the
fact was the Iraqi leaders were not really free to say whatever
they wanted, because, even though we were not in Iraq, the
Mukhabarat had sent spies to monitor what they said and
write down every word whenever they spoke in public. We
spotted them wherever we went.

Ayatollah Hussein Al-Sadr was the main speaker at
Chatham House and after he had finished, the audience was
free to ask him questions. I immediately recognized one of
the people who stood up from my medical days. Known
to me as Dr Baker, the head of a London medical agency,
his Iraqi name was Dr Mowaffak Baqer al-Rubaie. As he
addressed the Ayatollah he was very emotional and said,
"You were my closest friend and I have not seen you for
over twenty years!" It was an emotional occasion as these
old friends were reunited.

The next significant meeting was at Lambeth Palace,
where we met the Archbishop of Canterbury, Dr George
Carey. I had previously met the Archbishop only briefly,
and had never had a substantial meeting with him, but this
one turned out to be crucial and was the beginning of an
important relationship that endures to this day. Later, in his
last week as Archbishop, he would chair the meeting that
produced our historic "Alexandria Declaration" for peace
in the Holy Land. Now retired, Lord Carey is central to
my ministry and is patron of our Foundation for Relief and
Reconciliation in the Middle East.

Altogether, the visit of the Iraqi religious leaders was
highly significant in many ways, not least because it had a

major impact on how our ministry of reconciliation was perceived by others.

* * *

As the years went by, my reconciliation work in the Middle East expanded to a number of other nations and I began working in Jordan, Lebanon, and also Egypt. Each of these was a host nation for various major, life-changing reconciliation projects.

One such initiative was the effort to facilitate a meeting between Israeli and Palestinian leaders. Throughout all of the Middle Eastern conflict there had never been any serious engagement between opposing sides at a religious level, but I wanted to see the rabbis, priests, and imams agreeing to work together for peace. Achieving this was, of course, an incredibly delicate, complex task. I therefore began visiting the leaders of the various communities to canvass their opinions on whether they thought such a meeting was essential. After a number of initial discussions it seemed clear that there was the collective will to meet and talk. I felt that if a meeting of such gravitas were to take place, we would need a highly respected major leader to chair it. Owing to the nature of the meeting it would ideally be someone who was a Christian, rather than a Jew or a Muslim. I could think of no better person than the Archbishop of Canterbury, Dr George Carey.

On my return to the UK I went to see the Archbishop and asked him whether he would chair this important meeting of Israeli and Palestinian religious leaders. It was so encouraging to receive his positive response. I then returned to Israel and Palestine to take things further. I now needed to get the political leaders on board as well, as is usual in such initiatives.

The first person I went to see was Yasser Arafat. By now we had a very good relationship, had met regularly, and had discussed issues relating to the peace process on many occasions. I put the proposal to him in depth. Also in attendance was Saeb Erekat, the chief negotiator and head of the peace talks. It was clear that Yasser Arafat was totally behind the initiative and thought that it was just what was needed.

After this I needed to speak to the Israelis. It was decided that I should approach the Foreign Ministry to discuss the project, not least because the foreign minister himself was also a religious leader, Rabbi Michael Melchior. Not only did Rabbi Melchior support the initiative, but it was clear that he wanted to be actively involved in every aspect of the event.

My team and I therefore began to plan a series of meetings, out of which we would draft a joint statement from all the religious leaders. It was important that, as well as brokering a meeting between representatives of each side, we should make a tangible declaration of our collective commitment to peace and reconciliation. It was clear that we had broad Palestinian and Israeli support to do so.

In every aspect of our reconciliation work I have always sought to work closely with the British government, and so we wanted to work on the declaration in the British Embassy in Israel. Our British Ambassador in Tel Aviv at the time was Sherard Cowper-Coles. He had not been in office very long when I went to see him to discuss the project. In the midst of our conversation he stopped me and said, "I know you, don't I?" I told him I didn't think we had met before, and then he said, "We have. I came to see you about a parking problem at our home in Clapham. You were a councillor, weren't you?" It was a strange introduction to a man who would become a close friend and colleague!

CHAPTER 13

The Road to Alexandria

Preparation for the meeting to bring together the religious leaders continued night and day. Having received positive commitments from leaders on both sides of the divide, my next task was to find the right venue. We could not meet in Israel or on Palestinian National Authority (PNA) land – we needed somewhere nearby that was neutral, where both sides would be allowed to go. That didn't leave many options.

One possibility was Egypt. Both Israelis and Palestinians were allowed in and I had recently become friends with a significant Egyptian leader, Dr Ali Al-Samman, a government advisor who was also the interreligious advisor to Sheikh Tantawi, the Grand Imam of the Al-Azhar Mosque in Cairo.

Dr Ali and I travelled around Egypt looking for an appropriate venue, beginning in Cairo. There we also met with and consulted the Anglican bishop, the Most Revd Dr Mouneer Hanna Anis, and Osama El-Baz, who was a senior advisor to President Mubarak. Through Osama El-Baz we were able to secure the support of the Egyptian government.

As usual, I also sought to liaise with the British Embassy in Egypt, so I contacted the British Ambassador, Sir John

Sawers. John was very supportive and became intimately involved with our work.

After consulting these different parties it was decided that it would be better to hold such an important meeting outside Cairo, so we travelled for several hours south to Alexandria to look at venues there. The consensus was that this would be a more suitable location. We quickly found the perfect place in the Montazah Palace Hotel, which provided all the facilities we would need in considerable luxury. Bishop Mouneer, Ambassador Sawers, and Dr Ali all agreed that it was the ideal venue.

I could see that this whole venture was going to be hugely expensive to facilitate. How does one raise that kind of money? I had always been good at raising funds for ministry work, but to bring together and accommodate all the key religious leaders from both Israel and Palestine was a venture on an entirely different scale. I was reliant on God for His help. I knew that I could accomplish such a task only with the help of the Almighty, but I believed that God would provide what I needed; He had consistently done so in the past. I therefore committed the venture to Him in prayer: "Jesus, I love you so much. Will you provide all the money I need? I thank you and praise you that you always provide what I need."

It was a very simple prayer, but then all my prayers are simple. I have never prayed long and complicated prayers in times of need, always simple ones, with faith. I believe in spending much time with God, but He is our Father and knows our needs before we ask Him. We don't need to have long, drawn-out times of pleading with the Lord to provide for our needs. It is good to remain childlike before Him, especially in times of need.

God had already shown me wonderful provision for this venture in the shape of a gifted assistant who would be my "armour bearer" throughout the process. Tom Kay-Shuttleworth was a well-educated young man, having studied at Eton and Cambridge, and was a person of great character and integrity. His father was Lord Shuttleworth, a hereditary peer. While I provided the vision and personal contacts for this venture, Tom dealt diligently with all the details, in Israel and Palestine as well as Egypt.

Having the Archbishop of Canterbury present as chair of this historic meeting meant that we needed to secure the presence of equally senior Muslim and Jewish religious leaders. So my next task was to get the Grand Imam Tantawi on board. After several meetings and much discussion he agreed to attend, and this strengthened the importance of the meeting considerably. Following on from this I was able to secure the presence of the Sephardi Chief Rabbi of Israel, Eliyahu Bakshi-Doron. Things were looking very positive. When I eventually returned to Israel there was much joy among my colleagues that we had been able to secure the cooperation of Sheikh Tantawi and had found a suitable venue. The next difficult task would be to arrange a date that everyone could agree on.

It took a considerable time, amid his very busy schedule, to pin down a date that suited the Archbishop of Canterbury, but although he was incredibly busy, he made this a priority and I began to make the final arrangements for the big day.

* * *

Eventually the day came for us to travel to the Holy Land. We flew to Israel initially and the plane journey provided me with the perfect opportunity to brief the Archbishop fully on each of the delegates. We arrived in Tel Aviv and were greeted on the runway by the British Ambassador, Sherard Cowper-Coles, who guided us through the airport via the VIP route. This was a way into Israel that I had certainly not experienced before.

Once in Jerusalem we met some of the delegates who would be accompanying us and the British Ambassador handed us over to Geoffrey Adams, Britain's Consul-General in Jerusalem and the man responsible for Britain's relationship with the Palestinians. After a brief dinner together we were taken to Ramallah under heavy diplomatic escort to see Yasser Arafat, now a good friend of mine. This meeting was very productive, and Arafat made it clear what he expected to be achieved by our venture. No meeting remotely like this had occurred before, and he was keen to be a part of the initiative.

Early the next morning it was back to the Israeli side, to be accompanied by Sherard Cowper-Coles to a meeting with Israeli Prime Minister Ariel Sharon and Foreign Minister Shimon Peres. As we waited outside the prime minister's office, Tom Kay-Shuttleworth turned to me and said, "I am just about to enter probably the most important meeting of my life and I'm only twenty-three!" I was only just over ten years older myself, but I sensed this would be one of many such meetings in the future. This was the very thing that God had called me to do. It was a strange and different type of ministry – not the usual teaching- and preaching-based activity that most priests engage in – but I knew that the Lord's hand was guiding me.

THE DECLARATION

For our various meetings we had produced a draft statement – a declaration of our commitment to peace as a group of religious leaders working in cooperation. To cut a long story short, this took many hours of hard negotiation to achieve and it was not without its problems. At one point it looked as though the whole process would be derailed over one point. There was a request for a *hudna* – an Arabic word meaning "calm" or "quiet" – in other words, a ceasefire. This was viewed as merely a temporary measure by much of the Jewish delegation and so was opposed. Then, at the eleventh hour, just before we were due to have a press conference, Ambassador Sawers came to the rescue and we were able to replace the call for a *hudna* with the implementation of the "Mitchell and Tenet accords" – a set of recommendations outlined by Senator George Mitchell, champion of the peace process in Northern Ireland, and CIA Director George Tenet. We had finally completed the First Alexandria Declaration of the Religious Leaders of the Holy Land and this is how it read:

The First Alexandria Declaration of the Religious Leaders of the Holy Land

In the Name of God who is Almighty, Merciful and Compassionate, we, who have gathered as religious leaders from the Muslim, Christian and Jewish communities, pray for true peace in Jerusalem and the Holy Land, and declare our commitment to ending the violence and bloodshed that denies the right to life and dignity.

According to our faith traditions, killing innocents in the name of God is a desecration of his Holy Name, and defames religion in the world. The violence in the Holy Land is an evil which must be opposed by all people of good faith. We seek to live together as neighbours, respecting the integrity of each other's historical and religious inheritance. We call upon all to oppose incitement, hatred and the misrepresentation of the other.

1. The Holy Land is Holy to all three of our faiths. Therefore, followers of the divine religions must respect its sanctity, and bloodshed must not be allowed to pollute it. The sanctity and integrity of the Holy Places must be preserved, and freedom of religious worship must be ensured for all.

2. Palestinians and Israelis must respect the divinely ordained purposes of the Creator by whose grace they live in the same land that is called Holy.

3. We call on the political leaders of both peoples to work for a just, secure and durable solution in the spirit of the words of the Almighty and the Prophets.

4. As a first step now, we call for a religiously sanctioned cease-fire, respected and observed on all sides, and for the implementation of the Mitchell and Tenet recommendations, including the lifting of restrictions and a return to negotiations.

Our wedding day in 1991. From left to right: my parents Maurice and Pauline White; our best man, the Revd Richard Coombs; and Caroline's parents Peter and Mary Spreckley.

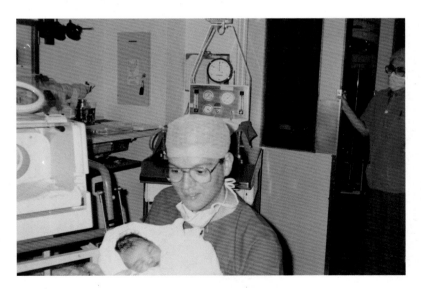

1986, during my medical career: I had just helped deliver this baby by caesarean section.

Punting the boys down the Cam beside Queen's College, Cambridge. Twelve years later Josiah is now a student at Queen's.

Introducing Caroline to Pope John Paul II in 1993.

The signing of the historic Alexandria Declaration. Seated: the then Grand Imam of the Al-Azhar Mosque, Mohammed Sayed Tantawi, and to his right the then Sephardi Chief Rabbi Bakshi-Doron. Standing behind them, from left to right: Sheikh Talal Sider, founder of Hamas; Chief Rabbi Michael Melchior, then deputy Foreign Minister of Israel; the assistant to the Chief Rabbi; the Most Revd George Carey, Archbishop of Canterbury; and Andrew White.

Standing amid the ruins of Coventry Cathedral: the first time the Iraqi religious leaders visited us at Coventry in 1999. From left to right: Fr Philip, a Chaldean priest; the Grand Ayatollah Hussein Al-Sadr; the late Chaldean Patriarch Raphael Bidawid; Andrew White; Sheikh Abdul Latif Humayem, formally Saddam Hussein's imam, now the head of the Sunni Wakf, and still a very close colleague.

Caroline and me with Prime Minister John Major.

With George Carey, Archbishop of Canterbury, and Prime Minister Tony Blair.

Presenting a bottle of HP sauce to Tariq Aziz, Deputy Prime Minister under Saddam Hussein, who first got me into Iraq.

I gave the Coventry Cross of Nails to Archbishop Desmond Tutu during a visit to the Holy Land in 2000.

With Sir Richard Branson at Coventry Cathedral, 2001. He worked closely with us on various reconciliation projects.

Above: He used to be my enemy, but he became a close friend: President Yasser Arafat, the leader of the Palestinian National Authority until 2005. One of my regular meetings with him along with my then project officer at Coventry Cathedral, Oliver Scutt.

Left: With my then co-director of the International Centre for Reconciliation at Coventry Cathedral, Justin Welby, now the Archbishop of Canterbury, on the day we reopened St George's Baghdad after the war in 2003. With us are the caretaker of St George's, Hanna Toma, and his daughter.

Right: Caroline and me at the launch of the Foundation for Relief and Reconciliation in the Middle East (FRRME) at the House of Lords in 2003.

Below: The Hasidic Rabbi Shimon Naftalis is very dear to me: he was my teacher when I was at Yeshiva, and is still my friend and colleague.

Right: Hundreds stand in line to receive food relief after church in 2005 at St George's, Baghdad.

Left: Dr Sara Ahmed is our inspirational director of operations. She has left her work in our clinic in Baghdad and is personally heading up all of our work amongst Internally Displaced People, the IDPs, in Northern Iraq. She herself is a Muslim, but is caring for the Christians and other minorities who have lost everything. True reconciliation in practice.

Below: J.John, Killy John, Caroline, Josiah, Jacob, and me together on their first and only visit to Erbil in what I call "pretend Iraq": Kurdistan, 2012.

Top: Two of the most important people in my life: my elder son Josiah with my dearest goddaughter Hannah-Rivkah, before I baptized her in the River Jordan.

Right: A normal day in war-torn Baghdad. On my rounds, wearing my body armour.

5. We seek to help create an atmosphere where present and future generations will coexist with mutual respect and trust in the other. We call on all to refrain from incitement and demonization, and to educate our future generations accordingly.

6. As religious leaders, we pledge ourselves to continue a joint quest for a just peace that leads to reconciliation in Jerusalem and the Holy Land, for the common good of all our peoples.

7. We announce the establishment of a permanent joint committee to carry out the recommendations of this declaration, and to engage with our respective political leadership accordingly.

There was much joy that we had finally achieved our goal. Following our meeting with Ariel Sharon and Shimon Peres, there was one last thing I needed to do, and that was to secure Yasser Arafat's approval of the final document. It was afternoon by now, the time when Arafat had a regular sleep. A few days before this I had disturbed his nap to discuss an important issue with him and had promised never to do it again, but we were soon to go before the world's media with news of the declaration and we had not yet run it by the Palestinian leader. So once again I had to ask for Arafat to be woken from his sleep to see me. Fortunately, he approved the declaration.

It had been incredibly difficult to reach this point. The meetings had been tense and the discussions heated and controversial. The thing that kept us going was that we all knew we had to achieve *something* from these historic discussions. No one wanted to leave the table empty-handed. Our meetings had brought together senior Orthodox Jewish rabbis with senior Islamic leaders, including one of the founders of the Islamic militant movement Hamas. Achieving an accord had been nothing short of miraculous. You can read more about the meeting between the religious leaders in my book *The Vicar of Baghdad*.[8]

* * *

From Alexandria we returned via Cairo, where we stopped off to see President Mubarak. We showed him the final declaration and he expressed significant pleasure in what had been achieved. It was a hugely encouraging sign that there was hope for peace and that we were moving in the right direction. Then, as we arrived back in Israel and were approaching Jerusalem, a huge bomb exploded in the city. It was a reminder of the fact that there was still a huge amount of reconciliation work to do and that the situation remained very volatile.

It was decided that we would form the Permanent Committee for the Implementation of the Alexandria Declaration (PCIAD) and that at least once a month I would chair a group in Jerusalem. There was much work to do and the Second Intifada (Palestinian uprising against Israel) still continued in the background, so we were working against the backdrop of a real crisis. Despite all this we persevered, and kept looking for ways in which we could practically demonstrate peace and support. We launched many initiatives to show that we were utterly committed to peace in action. Reconciliation was the only way forward.

---

8   Published by Monarch Books, 2009.

CHAPTER 14

Relief and Reconciliation Go Hand in Hand

I had had links with the Syrian Orthodox Christian community in Bethlehem since my student days. (While studying in Israel I'd lived in Old Jerusalem, opposite a tailor's shop run by Sami Barsoum, the lay leader of the whole Syrian Orthodox Community in Israel and the PNA, and I used to visit him to have my clothes specially made. I don't think there were too many of my contemporaries who had their own tailor!) I had a good friend called Joseph in Bethlehem, who was a carpenter by trade, just like another Joseph from Bethlehem a long time ago. Joseph had a young daughter, Despina, who suffered from a serious congenital illness called Marfan syndrome – a genetic disorder that affects the body's connective tissue. As a result she needed major spinal and other surgery.

There was no way that Joseph could find the thousands of dollars needed for this surgery, and the Lord gave me great compassion for him and his family. I therefore promised that somehow I would raise the necessary funds for them, which I did. It dawned on me then that the works of reconciliation and relief go together, hand in hand. A demonstration of practical love and care will often open the door to peacemaking. Despina had her surgery and recovered well. Twelve years later she is a close friend of mine and is about to graduate with a nursing degree from Bethlehem University.

Following this, I sought to establish a means of practical help for many other people – mainly Palestinians from very poor backgrounds. One day I asked Joseph if there was anything else that his community really needed, and his response was very clear – they were in desperate need of a school.

If I agreed to help this would, of course, be a major project, but I was very committed to doing whatever needed to be done. At this time I was still chairing one of the sections of the Barnabas Fund charity, providing help for suffering Christians. The Christians of Bethlehem could certainly be seen as a suffering minority who experienced a great deal of hardship, so I took the request to my colleagues at the Fund and they agreed to support the initiative, as did the churches of Coventry.

A major difficulty with any such project is that of finding an appropriate building. I spent a lot of time looking at many possible solutions, but it seemed that there were no premises available that would be usable immediately. We decided, therefore, that we must buy a building and adapt it to the unique needs of a school. Joseph and I travelled all around Bethlehem and the surrounding area and looked at many buildings. Eventually, in the next town, Beit Jala, we found a large, single-storey house with lots of potential and, importantly, room to expand. We bought the property and started making plans for its development.

The resulting school would belong to the Syrian Orthodox community and would be named the Mar Ephrem Christian School, after St Ephrem the Syrian, the fourth-century theologian. The purchase of the building heralded a time of great joy for the whole community.

An architect called Ghrassam, who lived in the community, was appointed to oversee the project and before long major development work commenced. The school began to take shape before our eyes, but not without difficulty. The Second Intifada continued and Beit Jala was far from being a peaceful place. I recall one day sitting on the school's roof, observing the work, when a bullet whipped past me. It was a sobering reminder of the dangerous conditions we were working in. Not long after that, Ghrassam himself was tragically killed in the violence. I was heartbroken. But even in the face of such desperate circumstances I was committed to completing the project, and before long work recommenced.

On one occasion I was leading a Holy Land pilgrimage group from Coventry and I took them to visit the school. Everyone was very enthusiastic about the project and they decided to form a committee to help support the school. To this day they are still going strong and are continuing to support what they call the "Bethlehem School Project".

Finally, with much celebration, the school was opened. It began with just fifteen pupils, but today has over 400. The very first pupils who arrived aged three are soon to graduate, now aged eighteen. The school is bursting at the seams and is now looking to expand to a new site on some land opposite the existing one. It is brilliant to see this dynamic institution going from strength to strength.

Serious reconciliation work must include helping those we are seeking to work with. If we can provide for their needs, the process of reconciliation can move forward more easily. In due course I would set up a foundation to support this type of ministry work and call it the Foundation for Relief and Reconciliation in the Middle East, because at the heart of our work in this region is simple provision for those in need.

An urgent summons

My life and work split between Coventry and the Holy Land continued. Having been diagnosed with MS three years earlier I had been managing well, but one day all my symptoms returned with a vengeance and my consultant decided that I needed to be admitted to hospital for a course of intravenous steroids.

As I lay in my hospital bed feeling terrible, my phone rang and on the other end was Yasser Arafat, telling me in a shuddering voice that he needed my help as his "church" had "been taken". It took me a while to understand what he was saying, but eventually I realized it was something to do with the Church of the Nativity in Bethlehem being under siege. I tried to explain to him that at that precise moment there was nothing I could do, as I was ill in hospital. I hung up, but then a few minutes later the phone rang again. This time it was Rabbi Michael Melchior.

Rabbi Michael's approach was typically direct, in true Israeli fashion: "I told you not to leave last week," he began. "We need you back, quickly!" I tried to tell him that I was ill in hospital, but he simply said, "Come back, now!" I hung up. Two minutes later my phone rang again. This time it was the Archbishop of Canterbury, who also urged me to get back to Israel. I saw no alternative but to discharge myself from hospital. Within minutes I was on my way out and within the hour had arranged to fly to Israel that night.

On arrival I tried to ascertain what was happening and what needed to be done. The situation was extremely complicated. A large group of terrorists had moved into Manger Square in the centre of Bethlehem. The Israeli army had tried to move them and they had ended up taking refuge in the Church of the Nativity. The army had surrounded the church, but did not want to go into it. Geoffrey Adams, the British Consul-General, told me that he wanted me to negotiate an end to the stand-off. It was clear that this would not be a straightforward process.

Both the Israelis and the Palestinians put forward negotiating teams and I was the only person allowed to be involved in both teams. We then spent several days discussing how the negotiations would be handled. It seemed clear that I was the only person both sides trusted. But the problem was far bigger than the present stand-off: the whole of Bethlehem had been placed under a curfew and that meant that, immediately, people were suffering from a lack of food and essential medical treatment. We needed to get food and medical supplies to those who needed it before we resolved our negotiations.

On this occasion I had with me my assistant, Alex, and my driver, Hanna. I decided that we needed to take immediate action about the food crisis and so we went shopping and bought a huge amount of food. We then had the potential problem of getting the food back through the checkpoint and into the neediest areas. But, as it happened, the commander in charge of Bethlehem at that time was a man with the wonderful name of Shmuley Hamburger. I knew him well and it was he who was manning the checkpoint. I explained the situation to him and we were allowed through. We then sought out the neediest people in the affected community – those who were struggling to survive. There was absolutely no one on the streets apart from Alex, Hanna, and myself.

Just as the local community was suffering, so were the priests who ran the Church of the Nativity complex. No supplies had been allowed in. With Shmuley Hamburger's help, I managed to get food to them. Shmuley and his troops delivered it themselves. I asked Shmuley if the priests had been happy with their food and he told me there had been a problem: I had forgotten to give them some lemons. I made a mental note that, if I ever distributed food to the people of the Middle East again, I would remember the lemons!

The negotiations were long and difficult. I was not the only expat in on them: there was another Englishman helping, also sent by the Consul-General. His name was Alistair and I was told he also worked for the Foreign and Commonwealth Office. Alistair quickly made it clear to me that he was not FCO staff but actually worked for MI6, and was one of their top hostage negotiators. We became great friends and I learned a lot from him. Hostage negotiation was something that would become a regular feature of my future reconciliation work, so, looking back now, I am grateful for Alistair's wisdom and insight.

A base for negotiations was set up in the home of the Palestinian Minister of Tourism in Beit Jala, next to Bethlehem. The negotiations involved detailed discussions about what would happen to those presently controlling the church. We had one man in the church with whom we were allowed to communicate, and then representatives of the Israeli military outside. The talks went on for days. The situation became seriously inflamed when we discovered that some of the hostages had been killed and their bodies stored in the Grotto of the Nativity. So then we had to negotiate to be allowed to retrieve the victims' bodies. Eventually this happened and then we resumed talks to get everyone freed.

One of the most difficult aspects of the whole operation was finding out the identities of the people inside the church. Once we discovered who they were, the Israeli army carried out a full intelligence briefing on each person. There were about 200 people in the complex, but around twenty of them were revealed to have significant terrorist histories. Of all the people inside, some would be allowed to return to their homes in the West Bank and others would be expelled to Gaza, but these twenty or so would need to go to other nations. We were now faced with the immense challenge of finding countries willing to admit known terrorists as residents. As you can imagine, countries were not queuing up to take them in.

I did, however, have a close relationship with a man called Miguel Moratinos, who at that time was the European Union's representative in the Holy Land. I therefore started the process of working through Miguel to try to find some European nations willing to take in some terrorists. It was a challenge that drove me to prayer, because only with God are such things possible. As in so much of my work, supernatural intervention is needed to get things done. Things that, on the face of it, seem utterly impossible.

A few countries were found, such as Spain, Italy, and Ireland. It looked as if we were finally getting to the end of the negotiations. Thirty-eight days had gone by and the hostages were still being held in the church. Finally, arrangements were made for each group of people to be taken by coach to a specific destination. We were nearly there. The transportation was due to arrive in the early hours of the morning and had been arranged by the US Embassy. We expected the handover to happen at about 2.00 a.m. We all stood waiting in Manger Square, but we were still there at 7.00 a.m. with no sign of anything happening, and had to give up.

Another day of negotiations took place to see what had gone wrong and what we could do now. Then in the early hours of the next morning we were back again, waiting for the hostages to come out. This time it happened as planned. After almost forty days the siege was over and the curfew was lifted. I could return to the UK.

Though it was wonderful to get back home to my family, I suddenly realized how traumatized I had been by this whole event. I had been immersed in this complex process for over a month and hadn't had time to process it for myself. Then, as I walked down the street in Coventry, I was stunned by the number of people who stopped to congratulate me on what I had achieved. I hadn't realized that the siege had been constantly in the media and had been very high-profile.

To my even greater surprise, a local boy told me that I must come to his house and see his bedroom. I went round to visit his family and saw that his bedroom walls were plastered with newspaper coverage of the event. I looked through the various reports and understood the magnitude and seriousness of what had taken place. I congratulated this young man on his spectacular collection, made my excuses, and left for home. As I walked back, I burst into tears and all my suppressed emotions came flooding out. I realized that from now on my life would be a bittersweet mixture of agony and ecstasy, of terrible lows as well as joyous highs. I wondered whether I could really live with such trauma.

My dear friend Bishop Colin Bennetts realized the enormity of what I had experienced. I confess that I went to see him unannounced, held him tight, and once again cried and cried. He understood the intensity of the pain I was feeling and provided great love and direction. He suggested that I go to see a professional counsellor in the diocese. I did, but to be honest they could not understand what I had experienced at all. This whole experience, however, helped me to see my own fallibility and vulnerability – and how much I must rely on God for His grace and power in my life. Apart from Him, I could do nothing.

CHAPTER 15

Back to Coventry

I spent a total of seven years in Coventry. It was a highly varied and always intense experience, during which I was privileged to travel the world and see things I never dreamed I'd see. But there was one challenge I faced that was perhaps greater than any other. It was not grasping incredibly complex political and religious relationships or even having to deal with terrorists. Rather, it was the challenge of travelling so much while my two boys grew up. Constantly being on the move is a wrench, but I accept the responsibilities of my role and so have to live with its consequences. Thankfully, my boys are blessed with an incredible mother in Caroline and whenever I am at home we always try to make the best of our time together. Both my boys are wonderful characters and there are numerous stories I could tell about them from this period of my life, but a few stand out in my mind.

My installation at Coventry Cathedral had brought together friends and family from far and wide. Caroline's wider family had historic links to the West Midlands, though we didn't know too much about them. But, as is inevitable at such events, people talked about their families and it wasn't long before we had discovered a lot about its many branches. Surprisingly, we had a historic connection to the Chamberlain family. Joseph Chamberlain was a well-respected politician and held the offices of both Chancellor of the Exchequer and Colonial Secretary. Less accepted was his son, Neville Chamberlain, prime minister before Winston Churchill. Neville Chamberlain was famous for declaring "Peace in our time" following the Munich Agreement of 1938, only for the nation to be thrust into war less than a year later.

I mention this because when my older boy, Josiah, was about seven years old, I asked him one day what he wanted to do when he grew up. He was very clear about his life plan: "I'm going to go to Cambridge and then I will leave and become prime minister." I enquired whether there would be a gap between his leaving Cambridge and starting work as prime minister, and he assured me there would not. Then he told me that since we'd never had a good prime minister in our family (referring to Chamberlain), he was going to be the first one! He had absorbed this information from the various conversations we'd had at my installation ceremony.

My boys have never known what it is like to have a father who does not travel all the time, so from the earliest age my frequent absence was completely normal for them. On one occasion I had been back home for about a week when Josiah observed, "Well, Daddy, it is time you went back to work now!" He had no concept of the fact that I could be working and still be in the country at the same time.

During the boys' early years I was still able to do most things that fathers do – such as participate in their children's sports days. I remember once taking part in a race where the fathers had to run carrying their sons. I was overjoyed when

Josiah and I won. Sadly, it was to be the last sports-day race I would take part in.

When away, I would speak to Caroline and the boys every day and they would inform me about what they had been studying in school. One day Josiah told me that he had been learning about stamps and commented that the Queen's head appeared on every stamp. Next came the question: would I take him to meet the Queen one day? This is not the type of request that most fathers are able to consider, let alone grant, but I promised Josiah that if I ever had the chance to meet the Queen I would do my best to ensure that he came with me. It was nothing short of a miracle that the very next day I received an invitation from Buckingham Palace to attend a lunchtime reception with the Queen. I phoned to accept and asked if it was possible for me to bring my young son, rather than my wife. I was told that the Queen loved children and that would be fine.

Next I had to speak to Josiah's school and ask permission for him to have a day off to meet the Queen. It was a rather strange conversation that I'm sure the school staff didn't have every day, but permission was granted on one condition – that he go wearing his smart school uniform. So, when the day came, Josiah travelled into London with me, correctly dressed and very excited. For the previous two weeks he had been practising how to say "Good morning, Your Majesty" and shake hands correctly. Accompanying us on the trip would be the Cardinal Archbishop of Westminster, so Josiah had also practised saying, "Greetings, Your Eminence" – which was altogether trickier for a small boy to accomplish.

At the lunch, Josiah was very taken with the idea of being inside a palace and eventually the Queen came along to greet each of her guests. She spoke to me and then I introduced her to Josiah. He spoke to her beautifully, bowed, and shook her hand in the way he'd practised. Her Majesty was obviously impressed and told him that he was very good at shaking hands. She then said that her grandchildren were not as good at shaking hands with people and she had to tell them that people had sweets in their hands in order to persuade them to do it. Josiah assured her that he was not like that!

As we left Buckingham Palace after the wonderful lunch and meeting, Josiah shocked me by asking if we could go to McDonald's next. I told him he'd just had a very nice lunch with the Queen.

"I know, Daddy," he responded. "It was very nice going to the Palace, but they didn't have any chicken nuggets or chips." I realized that for a young boy, meeting the Queen was all very well, but if she couldn't provide chicken nuggets and chips...!

My younger boy, Jacob, grew up with a bizarre understanding of international affairs for someone his age. Even before he was five he had an awareness of the kind of issues his daddy was involved in. In particular, like me, Jacob was fascinated with the Middle East. I remember when it was just coming up to his fifth birthday. He had already been attending school for a year and I asked him who he would like to have to come to his birthday party. He responded immediately by saying he wanted my "friend" to come. I asked him which particular friend he meant, though I had my suspicions, and he confirmed that it was Yasser Arafat, whom Jacob always referred to as "Yes Sir Arafat". Each night before bed, Jacob would say his prayers and, without fail, pray for, "Mummy, Daddy, and Yes Sir Arafat." I had to tell Jacob that it might be difficult for Yasser Arafat to come to his party at the moment, as he was locked up in his compound and could not go anywhere. But I said that Jacob should write Arafat a letter and I would give it to him the next week, when I was due to go back to the Holy Land.

The next week was a difficult one in the Middle East. The Second Intifada continued and most of the West Bank was off limits owing to increased violence. I was the only person allowed into Ramallah to visit Yasser Arafat. I typically met him for about an hour each week, but this day our meeting went on for much longer, covering a lot of political and religious ground. After three hours I was just about to leave when I suddenly remembered Jacob's letter, which was essentially an invitation to his party. I gave it to Arafat and relayed the story of how Jacob had so wanted him to come to his party, and how he prayed for him every single night.

Arafat was visibly moved by this and began to cry. "He really loves me," he said over and over, and I assured him that Jacob did indeed care deeply about him. Then Arafat called over one of his aides and sent him to fetch one of his *keffiyeh* – the distinctive patterned headdresses he always wore in public. He wrote on it in red pen, "To Jacob from Yasser Arafat".

I handed the *keffiyeh* to Jacob on his birthday and his eyes widened.

"This must be from Yes Sir Arafat," he exclaimed, and I confirmed it was. His other birthday present was a green army uniform, so he put on both items and looked just the part. However, the look wasn't quite satisfactory for Jacob. He clearly wanted to look *exactly* like Arafat, so he took the somewhat dramatic step of drawing a beard on his face with a thick marker pen! After this, the *keffiyeh* came out for successive Christmas nativity plays.

From this time forward, during my meetings with Yasser Arafat, he would frequently call Jacob for a chat. It was quite bizarre seeing this renowned international figure talking to a little boy in England. One Saturday evening, while I was back in England myself, Arafat phoned me at home. He said he wanted to have a chat with Jacob before he spoke with me. I called from my study, "Jacob, President Arafat's on the phone and wants to talk to you." Jacob shouted back, "Tell him I'm busy and I will call him later." He was watching *The Simpsons*.[9] Well, that's a child's perspective of what is important!

Growth of the International Centre for Reconciliation

Meanwhile, the work of the International Centre for Reconciliation (ICR) expanded in many different directions, meaning that my role as director grew ever more demanding. In order to cope with these demands, I increasingly leaned upon the Lord.

Whenever I was not travelling I shared in the running of one of Britain's most significant cathedrals and learned much from taking part in the daily liturgy, often accompanied by Coventry's outstanding choir. Some people think that sharing in such "professional" worship is far removed from a real encounter with the Almighty, but nothing could be further from the truth.

Time and again our Lord met with me in supernatural ways. He would speak to me and impart incredible wisdom for the situations I was involved in. I would be kneeling

---

9   *The Simpsons* is an American animated sitcom created by Matt Groening for the Fox Broadcasting Company.

quietly in my stall, in the midst of exquisite worship, and God would tell me what He wanted to do in Iraq, Israel, Palestine, or northern Nigeria. The words from the Communion liturgy became my reality: "The Lord is here; His Spirit is with us." Today, writing this in Baghdad, I declare this truth several times a day. It is God's very presence that sustains us through the most difficult and challenging of circumstances.

Although the Middle East remained the central focus of my work for the ICR, other areas of the world opened up that were also experiencing conflict. This was chiefly through the Community of the Cross of Nails (CCN), a worldwide community committed to reconciliation, established in 1940. In post-war years it was significant in healing the rifts between countries that had been in conflict, such as Britain and Germany. During my time in Coventry there were over 200 CCN centres around the world and some of my time was taken up visiting them.

Many of the European centres had either once been at war with the UK or caught up in the battles surrounding Communism. But other centres were being established in areas of new conflict, such as northern Nigeria – not least in the diocese of Kaduna, where my friend Josiah Idowu-Fearon was bishop.

Northern Nigeria was the scene of a growing conflict between Muslims and Christians. Our ICR team thought it wise for me to visit there to ascertain what might be done to establish a process of reconciliation. When I arrived, the situation was much more tense than I'd imagined. Hundreds were being killed on each side and both churches and mosques were being ransacked and destroyed.

I soon became friends with a Christian pastor called James, who was working closely with an Imam called Ashafa.

Together they had formed the Muslim–Christian Dialogue Forum to conduct talks between the conflicting groups and make an attempt at reconciliation. I was invited into this group and that was the beginning of a long, complex process within northern Nigeria.

On one of my early visits I was joined by a contact from my former Wandsworth Council days, fellow councillor Lola Ayorinde. Lola was a Nigerian Muslim and, since the days when we'd served together, had risen to the position of Mayor of Wandsworth. The fact that we were prepared to travel together into this place of conflict spoke loudly of our mutual commitment to peace. It also raised a considerable amount of interest among the locals – the fact that a Nigerian lady was the mayor of a part of London.

We stayed with Bishop Josiah. As was our practice, we divided our time between involvement in the serious political aspects of conflict negotiation and engaging with and supporting local churches. The churches were delighted to see us and were deeply concerned about the nature of the conflict. What was clear was that many Christians were involved in the conflict themselves and didn't intend to take lying down the aggression being shown towards them. There were as many who were prepared to fight back as there were committed to turning the other cheek.

Meetings between Muslim and Christian leaders were intense and inflammatory. Churches and mosques had been destroyed, religious seminaries burned to the ground, on both sides of the divide. We started from the ground up to try to establish how everyone might work together, to respect and learn from one another. The bridge that had been established by Pastor James and Imam Ashafa was a critical aspect of the discussions.

Over the following months I returned to Kaduna many times and we began working towards drafting a declaration for peace called the Kaduna Declaration. It was based on the Alexandria Declaration, but contextualized for northern Nigeria. In due course, after many meetings at both a local and a city-wide level, it was decided that the words of the declaration should be set in marble and stone and placed on the main roundabout at the entrance to the city. Several months after my first visit there, this symbol of reconciliation was unveiled by the state governor in an atmosphere of great joy.

* * *

While the ICR's reconciliation work became increasingly complex in different regions of the world, we began to think about how to marry up these different initiatives. Coventry did not have a partner diocese, so with Bishop Colin Bennetts' blessing it was decided that there should be formed a three-way partnership between the Diocese of Coventry, the Syrian Orthodox Diocese of Jerusalem and the Middle East, and the Diocese of Kaduna in Nigeria. These two dioceses were already Coventry's closest partners so it seemed appropriate, if all three bishops agreed, that a formal link be established.

After much discussion, everyone agreed that the official partnership should go ahead and a date and location were set for a celebration to mark the event. This would take place in St Mark's Syrian Orthodox Monastery Church in Jerusalem. St Mark's is the mother church of the Syrian Orthodox Church and the oldest church in the world. It stands on the ancient site of the house of Mary, mother of St Mark the Evangelist (Acts 12:12), according to a sixth-century inscription which was discovered in 1940, and it is traditionally held to be the place where the Last Supper took place in an upper room. That room is no longer above ground but underground, since the streets of first-century Jerusalem were at least twelve feet lower than they are today.

The ceremony eventually held there was a remarkable event. It was a hugely emotional moment when the Coventry cross of nails was placed on the altar in the ancient chapel of the upper room. To this day the cross of nails remains in this most hallowed site. When in Jerusalem I often just go and stand in this holy place and gaze at the cross, wrought from nails from the ruins of Coventry Cathedral, and in it see my whole life summed up.

As the work of the ICR became increasingly intense and hectic, it became clear that it was all too much for one person to handle. Bishop Colin was very happy with the way the work had developed, but thought that I needed another senior member of staff to work with me. Bishop Colin asked me if there was anyone in the diocese I would consider inviting on board as a co-director. There was one person I respected greatly, who had accompanied me on a previous trip to the Middle East – the vicar of Southam, Warwickshire, none other than Justin Welby, the present Archbishop of Canterbury. I could think of no one better suited to the role, and Bishop Colin agreed. In just a few weeks Justin had joined me as Co-Director of the ICR and it was wonderful having my friend share the work alongside me.

To start with, Justin travelled with me to visit all of our projects in Nigeria and the Middle East. Immediately he was at ease communicating with all the diverse groups we were working with, Jews, Arabs, and Nigerian Muslims and Christians, as well as our long-term colleagues in Europe and the US. After working together closely for a time, we knew that we must divide the work between us. It was clear that, owing to my historic and extensive connections in the Middle East, I should continue that work. In Nigeria the work was not as well established and Justin had already experienced working in Nigeria during his time in the oil industry, so it made sense for him to take the lead there.

Shortly after Justin came on board I felt it was time to take a long-overdue sabbatical. In truth, it wasn't a typical sabbatical – it was not to rest or do less work. Instead, I returned to my beloved Cambridge to take up residence as a visiting fellow at Clare College. I suppose it was a sabbatical in the sense that I was able to have a complete break from my usual work and focus on something different. It was wonderful to be back in the academic hothouse. I divided my time between teaching, studying, writing, and preaching. While there, I was able to write my first book about ministering in Iraq and my call to the ministry of reconciliation.

I remember one day standing up to give a lecture and looking out at the audience. I had been taught by the majority of the people I was about to address and I found it a very humbling experience. All I could think was, I am who I am today because of these great people.

CHAPTER 16

Brought Back to Life

After my first visit to Iraq, whenever I travelled there I made sure I paid a visit to St George's Anglican Church. I mentioned in Chapter 11 that the church had been looted and was lying derelict. Not a pew remained in the building – it was empty apart from the heavy marble font. There was obviously no market for fonts in Iraq.

The church had formerly been an active place of worship, serving the expat community until the Iraqi invasion of Kuwait in 1991. After that, Saddam Hussein had shut it down, because it had always been known as "the English church". The church was indeed English: the land and property belonged to the British Embassy, and therefore counted as a slice of British soil.

St George's was established in 1864 when missionaries from Christ Church, Jaffa Gate – the Anglican church located inside the Old City of Jerusalem – went to Baghdad. They began a ministry which eventually grew into St George's Church. It is significant to me that St George's came out of the ministry of Christ Church, Jaffa Gate, a church that is very important to me. Christ Church functions under the patronage of the Church's Ministry among Jewish People

(CMJ), of which I happen to be Vice-President. In so many ways my ministry began in Jerusalem and has ended up in Baghdad. I give the Lord thanks for the historical link between these two places that I love.

Clive Handford, the former Bishop of Cyprus and the Gulf, had put in place Hanna the caretaker to look after the building, and with the oversight of my aide in Iraq, Georges Sada, it was in much better shape by the time I visited it with a delegation of bishops. In a sense, St George's first official service took place on that trip with bishops Colin Bennetts, Peter Price, and Clive Handford. We celebrated Holy Communion and I prayed, "One day, Lord, may this church come alive again." So bleak was the situation for Christians in Iraq that essentially I was asking for the miracle of resurrection. But as we continued to pray I was struck again by that phrase from the Eucharistic Prayer, "The Lord is here; His Spirit is with us", and I thought, "Well, my God is rather good at resurrections!"

Justin Welby accompanied me to Iraq on my first visit there after the outbreak of war in 2003. I wanted to open St George's officially and felt strongly that somehow God would restore it to its former glory. We planned a service during which Justin would celebrate Communion and I would lead and preach. We invited Archbishop Mar Addi, leader of the Assyrian Church, to reconsecrate the church. We also invited John Sawers, British Ambassador in the Coalition Provisional Authority, to read one of the lessons, along with one of the US Army generals. There were still no pews in the building, but we had managed to buy enough plastic garden chairs for everyone to be seated.

The reading that day was a hugely significant one, from Haggai 2:9 (KJV):

The glory of this latter house shall be greater than of the former, saith the LORD of hosts: and in this place will I give peace, saith the LORD of hosts.

These words are inscribed on a tablet set into the face of the ruined tower of Coventry's old cathedral. Suddenly I could see their prophetic relevance in the place I was currently standing – St George's, ruined by war, just like Coventry, but with a more glorious future ahead. Was God telling me that St George's would be greater than it had ever been in the past? Greater than in the vibrant days of its foundation? I believed that was exactly what God was saying.

We held services for the following two weeks and people began to attend the church. Then the violence outside the secure Green Zone began to get worse, meaning that it was too risky for people to venture out to St George's to worship, and our numbers immediately diminished.

Determined to see the ministry of St George's resurrected, however, we moved our service to the chapel of the Republican Palace and into Saddam's former throne room. Interestingly, from that moment the local Iraqi Christians began to perceive that we were less affiliated with the Coalition than they had thought, and began to attend our services. The church grew quite rapidly from then on, multiplying by almost a hundred new people each week. After it had lain dormant for so long, suddenly we had a viable Iraqi church filled with people from every possible Iraqi denomination. There were no Anglicans, but there were Chaldeans, Assyrians, Armenians, Syrian Orthodox, Assyrian Catholics, and Presbyterians. At no time did we ever try to convert them to Anglicanism – we just made it clear to people that we were Christians and that we respected their immense spiritual heritage.

I myself had a great deal to learn about the Christian heritage of Iraq and it was a steep but exciting learning curve. I took our Anglican liturgy and contextualized it, taking account of Iraqi culture, so that it would be understandable to the average Iraqi. The hugely significant words from the Eucharistic Prayer, "The Lord is here; His Spirit is with us", became, in Arabic, *Allahu ma'ana*: "the Lord is here". This was the beginning of our Iraqi church.

Meanwhile, I continued to establish the wider work of reconciliation in the nation. A huge help in this was the head of the British Mission to Baghdad, a wonderful, experienced diplomat called Christopher Segar. He headed up what was called the BOB House (British Office Baghdad), which in essence functioned as a British Embassy. Christopher was a very helpful diplomatic colleague, but in due course also became a good friend. He would later become one of the trustees of my Foundation.

Christopher helped us immeasurably with our work in Iraq by always providing for us the right contacts at the right time. Although Georges Sada accompanied me constantly as I travelled around, I really needed another person with a diplomatic background who was able to translate for me. Christopher found me just the right person in Ambassador Sadoun al-Zubaydi. He had been Iraq's Ambassador to Indonesia, had a PhD from Birmingham University in England, and was an expert in Shakespeare! Having studied in the Midlands, he knew Stratford-upon-Avon very well, which happened to be in the Diocese of Coventry. What I didn't know about Sadoun when I first met him was that he had also been the senior translator for Saddam Hussein – so Saddam's translator became my translator!

GROWTH OF ST GEORGE'S MINISTRY

I was aware that St George's was supposed to be an Anglican church, despite the fact that none of the congregation were actually Anglicans. I thought about the different aspects of ministry that characterized the Anglican Church around the world and how they related to the needs of ordinary people. I had experienced the full dynamism of the Anglican Church in both Kenya and Nigeria, and in each case the Mother's Union (MU) had been one of the most prevalent ministries. I was, of course, aware of the organization in the UK and had even been a member myself (yes, men are allowed to be members of the MU!), but it had a much more active ministry in Africa.

I decided that we needed to establish a branch of the MU in Baghdad, which we did, and one of our ladies, Nawal, led the project. Within days of its beginning, the Baghdad MU had over 2,000 signed-up members and they set to work, worshipping the Lord together and going out into the community to care for the poor and suffering. We created a link between our branch of the MU and their headquarters in London. Our ladies were very excited about being part of an international movement.

MEETING PRACTICAL NEEDS

One day, I was standing in the grounds of the church, having one of my regular conversations with the Lord, and I was telling Him that the needs of our church people were huge. I asked, "Lord, what do I need to provide for our people?" His answer came back very clearly: people needed food, adequate healthcare, and an education for their children.

Each was a big area of need, but it was relatively easy to start with food. The MU played a key role in distributing food to those who most needed it. All of our congregation were issued with photo ID cards and a "distribution area" was created, so that each week after the main Sunday service food could be properly allocated to those in need.

Healthcare and education needs were more difficult to meet – especially the former. Already, large numbers of people were looking to the church to help them with their health problems. As the need arose, we paid for people to see doctors, have tests done, and obtain medication. But this policy was not sustainable for the long term. It was clear that it would be better to establish our own health centre.

We had one place in the church grounds that could be turned into such a facility – the old church hall, where Hanna the caretaker lived with his family. We found a new home for Hanna and his family and started planning the creation of a new health centre with several aspects. We needed an area for general practitioners to function, and also a dental clinic. Eventually we would also have a pharmacy, a laboratory, and a clinic for autologous stem-cell treatment (transplants using the person's own stem cells). It was a huge project, which, fortunately, the US Embassy agreed to both organize and fund. It was all overseen by Brigadier General David Greer, who today is the Executive Director of the US branch of my Foundation.

The clinic now treats over 150 people every day, and the treatments provided range from seeing the doctors and dentists to distributing medication from the pharmacy. Most of our patients are Muslims. In Iraq it is impossible to do any overt evangelism, but scores of people have joined St George's after receiving free treatment at our clinic. Our health centre is our biggest means of evangelism. The thing that distinguishes it from every other clinic in Baghdad is that it is completely free. The fact that it is located in the church complex follows the historical precedent set by the church throughout the ages, of offering a ministry of healing to all who need it.

Jesus is our model for all ministry and a key feature of His ministry was supernatural healing, so we not only aim to treat people with medicine, we also pray for everyone. Thus the ministry of the church is not restricted to the help that our clinic can supply; at its heart is the supernatural healing power of our Lord.

St George's has a very significant prayer ministry and people have a great expectation that, if they are prayed for, the Lord will meet with them and heal them. People regularly experience the reality of the Lord's power. The majority of the Muslims who visit our clinic hold the belief that if a priest anoints them with oil, they will be healed. Sadly, there is too much reliance on the ministry of the priest, instead of on a personal relationship with the Lord who supplies the power – and this is true of some of the Christians as well as the non-Christians.

Every Saturday afternoon, a group of our MU women go out visiting the poor and praying for those who are ill. They ask the Lord to heal everyone they meet. Each year at our diocesan synod, which meets in Cyprus, the bishop will bless the oil that all the churches in the diocese will use for anointing. We are given a fairly large bottle of oil. St George's is the only church in the world I know of that regularly runs out of oil – because we pray for so many people.

St George's is also the only church I know of where people regularly ask to take the sacraments away with them to minister to others. People ask for anointing oil, which is good because it means they are praying for healing for others. They also ask for Communion wafers for those who are too frail to come to church. They will take burnt-out candles, water from the font, and anything else they consider holy.

Some people may think this strange, yet every week I hear stories about what God has been doing in people's lives. There are stories of supernatural healing and of prayers for needs being miraculously answered. Then there are countless visions of Jesus, with people relaying to me what the Lord has said to them. It is truly remarkable what God is doing in the lives of ordinary Iraqis.

CHAPTER 17

An Oasis of Healing

Each Thursday evening at the church we meet to pray specifically for healing. Whenever I am there, people will expect to be anointed with oil. At these services we don't just pray for the people who are present; we keep a book listing the names of everyone who has requested prayer. This book is lifted up to the Lord in prayer with the assurance that He will indeed hear and answer these prayers. Each week after this meeting we hear more stories of how God has answered people's prayers, often with dramatic healing. We have seen people healed of heart disease and various cancers, and children healed of congenital illnesses. We have even seen the Lord raise people from the dead. Allow me to tell you about two such incidents.

One Saturday afternoon some ladies from our MU went to visit a pregnant lady who was ill in hospital. As they entered the ward, they saw another patient next to her crying hysterically. One of our ladies asked what was wrong with her and was told that her baby had just died and been taken down to the mortuary. Immediately our ladies asked if they could go there and see the baby. They were allowed to do this and were directed to the baby, who had been placed in one of the refrigerated units. One of the ladies took the lifeless child in her arms and they all began to pray that life would return to him. After a moment, the child opened his eyes and began to cry. They were able to carry the baby back to the ward and place him in the arms of his astonished and overjoyed mother. Now everyone was crying.

The next story is my favourite. Ahmed was a normal working man in Baghdad. He came to our clinic one day and pleaded with one of our doctors to treat his daughter. It turned out that his teenage daughter, Abouna, was seriously ill in Medical City, Iraq's main university hospital. He asked if our doctors would treat her because of the popular local belief that the so-called "English clinic" could cure anybody. Our doctors had to explain that, sadly, we could not treat someone who was already a patient of another hospital.

Ahmed was very distressed but there was nothing to be done, so one of our doctors suggested that he return to the hospital and visit his daughter. Before Ahmed left, however, I had the opportunity to speak to him and pray with him. As I did, I felt the Lord speak to me and I became utterly convinced that the Lord was going to heal this girl. I told Ahmed, "Go to the hospital now and pray for her. And, all the way there, just keep on saying 'Yeshua, Yeshua, Yeshua', continuously." ("Yeshua" is the Aramaic name for Jesus.)

Ahmed arrived at the hospital only to be greeted with the tragic news that his daughter had died minutes earlier. In desperation and with many tears, he went to her bedside and wrapped his arms around her body, saying "Yeshua" over and over again, just as I'd instructed him. His daughter immediately breathed out, sat up, and said, "Baba (Daddy), I'm hungry. Can I have some food?" Later, when Ahmed came to see me and tell me what had happened, I said to him, "Don't worry; it has happened before..."

Why not you?

As is so often the case in parts of the world where Christians are experiencing great hardship and persecution, or there is just great spiritual darkness, manifestations of the power and presence of God occur regularly. For us, here in Baghdad, we live daily with an awareness of the supernatural. One such manifestation is the appearance of angels. Western readers might find this hard to grasp, but here we see many angels.

One day, my adopted son, Dawood (you'll hear more about him in a later chapter), was trying to take some photos of me for one of my books, and he said, "Daddy, there are too many angels. They are getting in the way of the picture!" I told him to take the picture anyway and the result was extraordinary – I was clearly surrounded by what I would describe as glowing orbs of light.

Previously I was sceptical whenever I heard people talking about angelic encounters. Not that I didn't believe it could happen, but I like to check things out and make sure they are real. But now I have seen the angels for myself and I accept that, in a church where the miraculous is the norm and incredible healings take place, the presence of the Almighty and His angelic hosts is tangible, and sometimes even visible.

Whenever I travel and speak at different churches, I will usually mention some of these things, which frequently results in my being asked, "So why not you? Why have you not been healed?" I think this is a fair question: why am I still living with MS when God is obviously capable of healing me? With all my heart I believe that the Lord can heal me if He wants to, but at the same time I am acutely aware of how the Spirit of God has been with me constantly, miraculously enabling me to do everything I've ever needed to do.

I have known what it is to be so ill that I can hardly move, and yet here in Iraq, with its fairly primitive medical facilities compared with the Western world, at our own clinic in our own church the doctors have found a way of treating me with my own stem cells. Other people would travel around the world for such treatment, but I can walk down our church path. I was the first person to receive this treatment and it has totally transformed my life. We have since had people come from as far away as the USA to undergo similar treatment. Several thousand people have been treated and the condition of 80 per cent of them has radically improved. For this I so thank my God. Who would ever have thought that treatment for MS would be available at my church in Baghdad?

I give thanks for God's provision in this. At the same time, I feel great frustration at the bad counsel that has often been given to me by other Christians. People have told me that I haven't been healed because I've never really believed God enough for it – suggesting a deficiency in my faith. Others have told me that my view of God is too small, too limited – suggesting a deficiency in my understanding of the Almighty's power and sufficiency. I have heard these things time and time again. In addition, countless people have come to me saying that they are the one through whom I'll be healed. At least all of this has taught me how *not* to pray for people in need, and I have learned much about the never-failing love of God in our most difficult circumstances.

One thing I know for sure is that if God calls us to do something, He always enables us to do it, and He also gives joy in the doing. He who has called you will never fail you. I know without doubt the truths that, "my grace is sufficient for you, for my strength is made perfect in weakness" (2 Corinthians 12:9, NKJV) and "I can do all things through Christ who strengthens me" (Philippians 4:13, NKJV). The fact that God should use me and not someone who is a picture of good health to bring His healing to others is another sign of God's incredible grace. It's all about Him, not me.

GOD'S PRESENCE MANIFEST THROUGH OTHERS

There is so much need in this war-torn country of Iraq that we could not possibly carry on conducting this ministry without God's help – and so often that help is manifested through others. When we say, "The Lord is here; His Spirit is with us", we also think of so many friends around the world who support us in a multitude of ways. Like all churches in every land, the church here is not just about where the building is located.

One thing we do frequently in Iraq is to go and visit people in their homes – an experience that manages simultaneously to be both thrilling and devastating. Thrilling because the presence of God is always manifest and devastating because the people live in such extreme poverty. It is hard to describe the poor state of people's accommodation: damp, run-down buildings with peeling plaster, no proper floor surface, nothing to sit on, very little food – the list goes on and on. There is no such thing as a comfortable chair – most people just have to sit or lie on the floor, including some very disabled people. But, without exception, people are always delighted to see us and they say that when a priest visits them they are indeed visited by the Lord.

In our ministry to these people we are helped by so many other churches around the world that I must make mention of them. I realize that in mentioning some I may forget to mention others, and I hope that I don't offend anyone.

First of all, there is the "second" St George's – an extension of our main fellowship. Each Saturday I conduct a service based in the US Embassy complex – a large site covering 100 acres that I refer to as the largest prison in the world, since it is surrounded by a twenty-four-foot wall topped with razor wire and punctuated by military watchtowers. It is impossible to get into or out of the place unless you have security clearance at the highest level.

I conduct two services there: first a general, interdenominational service, and then a more traditional Anglican service. The congregation are not all Americans; about half come from Kenya and Uganda. This means we enjoy some wonderful African-style worship, with great joy and rhythm. This Embassy church also calls itself St George's, Baghdad because we are one, even though it is not possible for the whole church to gather together most of the time.

Once each year, however, at Christmastime, we do gather the church together as large numbers of our young people go to the Embassy to receive toys from the US Marines as part of their "Toys for Tots" programme. Throughout the rest of the year our Embassy congregation does what it can to support and provide help for the families we reach out to on a daily basis, enabling us to show them the love and care of God.

Then there are churches around the world that constantly support us. There are several in the US who, whenever I visit them, fuel my vision and courage for the work in Iraq. Pastor Kyle Horner is one such man, leader of Connect Church in Cherry Hill, New Jersey. I met Kyle not in America but in an Indian restaurant in Kent in the south of England. We were both preaching at the same conference and instantly clicked and became friends. Kyle and his wife Danielle's church is so alive and filled with the Spirit of God – they are a great inspiration to me.

I cannot think about churches in the US without thinking of the work of Bill and Beni Johnson at Bethel Church in Redding, California. To me, this church is like no other and has such an incredible emphasis on abiding in God's presence.

Then there are numerous churches in the UK: Holy Trinity Brompton where I have many friends; Cornerstone Church at Sandown Racecourse in Epsom, Surrey, led by my dear friend Pastor Chris Demetriou. There is Kerith Church in Bracknell, Berkshire, with its pastor, Simon Benham. Pastor Phil Whitehead at Chiswick Christian Centre is someone who never fails to truly inspire me in my mission. Finally, there is LIFE Church, Bradford. I have only been to this church twice, but each time I found it inspiring. I can guarantee that once each day I will hear from someone from at least one of these churches, and this does so much to encourage me to keep going.

Someone once said to me that going from our church in the war zone of Baghdad to Bethel Church must be like going from heaven to hell. I replied, "No, it's like going from one form of heaven to another." Why? Because we are both pursuing the call of the kingdom as laid out in Isaiah 61:1–4 (NIV):

> The Spirit of the Sovereign Lord is on me, because
> the Lord has anointed me to proclaim good
> news to the poor. He has sent me to bind up

the broken-hearted, to proclaim freedom for the
captives and release from darkness for the prisoners,
to proclaim the year of the Lord's favour and the
day of vengeance of our God, to comfort all who
mourn, and provide for those who grieve in Zion
– to bestow on them a crown of beauty instead
of ashes, the oil of joy instead of mourning, and a
garment of praise instead of a spirit of despair. They
will be called oaks of righteousness, a planting of
the Lord for the display of his splendour. They will
rebuild the ancient ruins and restore the places long
devastated; they will renew the ruined cities that have
been devastated for generations.

These words describe the sum total of what we are doing in
Baghdad and what the worldwide church as a whole should
be doing. This is our mission – the same mission as that of
Cornerstone Church in Cherry Hill and Bethel Church in
Redding. We may be conducting our ministry in the midst
of terror and the carnage of war, but we are still working
together with the wider church, proclaiming good news to
the poor, binding up the broken-hearted, and proclaiming
freedom for the captives and release from darkness for the
prisoners.

CHAPTER 18

Don't Take Care; Take Risks

President Jimmy Carter once said, "Go out on a limb – that's where the fruit is." I share his philosophy. I constantly say to people, "Don't take care; take risks." It has become my motto and the principle by which I live my life. Risk is inherent in most of my work. The fact is, if I weren't prepared to risk everything for the sake of peace, then very little would be achieved.

Recently, I was honoured to receive the William Wilberforce Award (given to individuals who "exemplify the passions and principles of Wilberforce as a witness of real Christianity in society"). When I arrived at the award ceremony, all the posters bore the words "Take Risks". People assumed those words came from me, but in fact they came from my great mentor, Donald, Lord Coggan.

Lord Coggan first uttered this statement to me as we were walking together in London. We had just come from a meeting of the Council of Jews and Christians and he gripped my arm tightly, looked me in the eye, and said, "You're a young curate. I want to give you just two words

169

of advice for your ministry: take risks." The weight of those words stayed with me.

Just a few weeks later I was in Rome, visiting Pope John Paul II in my capacity as chairman of the young leadership section of the International Council of Christians and Jews. I went for a walk with the Pope through the Vatican and, similarly, he turned to me and said, "You are at an early stage of your ministry. You will go far if you always take risks." I replied, "Yes, Your Holiness, I promise I always will." And this is what I have done throughout my ministry.

I know for a fact that, whenever I have decided not to take a risk, I have limited the work of the Holy Spirit. So, whenever the Lord has brought this to my attention, I've repented and next time been bolder in stepping out and trusting Him.

What risks do I take? I will talk about them in this chapter, but it occurs to me that whereas these areas of risk apply to my peculiar context, we all face the same risks, regardless of our walk in life, because they deal with the two greatest facets of our humanity: our relationship with God (and the degree to which we trust Him) and our relationships with one another. I summarize these risks as follows:

- The risk of loving
- The risk of asking much from God
- The risk of seeking reconciliation
- The risk of engaging with our enemies
- The risk of trusting God to keep us safe.

The risk of loving

To love is to risk

The act of demonstrating love to another is perhaps the greatest risk any of us will ever take, because it can be the most powerful thing, but is also fraught with danger. What if our love is rejected or misunderstood? What if our love is in vain or we have risked loving only to be used and then discarded?

At the start of this book I recalled how, from the earliest age, I was aware that Jesus loved me very much. So one of the first things I did was learn to love God back. Loving God is perhaps the only love without risk, because our Lord took all the risk upon Himself.

Loving other people, however, involves risk – yet God has called us to be people of love; to love others selflessly; to be the hands and feet of Jesus by showing practical love to those who need it. Of course, it is easier to love those who love us, but what about our enemies, those who despise us? This is the real risk of love: to love those who you know have no intention of loving you back. But still God commands us to love them, and His love is a powerful catalyst for change. The real risk in loving is to trust God that, as we simply love, He will take responsibility for the consequences.

Love involves pain

We know that love also involves pain. We choose to love someone, but they reject us. Someone we love deeply lets us down. The more we love someone, the more acutely we feel the pain when things go wrong. Perhaps the most difficult thing I have ever experienced in my ministry has been the pain of betrayal – loving people unconditionally only to have them turn on me or reject me.

But we have a choice in how we deal with the bitterness and anger that can arise from such pain. We can either build fences around ourselves, to prevent the situation from arising again, or risk loving once again and build a bridge, leaving a way open for that person to come back to us, should they choose to do so. We all know which choice we *should* make, with the Lord's help.

Love is a choice

Love itself is not just an emotion; it is an act of the will. Loving others is a choice. If we are real, practising Christians, we do not have the option of simply rejecting other people. If we do that, we are failing to practise our faith. I would dare to say that such an attitude brings us very close to no longer even *having* a faith. To turn on others in this way is no less than turning on God and rejecting Him. We can try to make excuses for our behaviour, but the truth is that we are commanded by God to love others as He has loved us.

THE RISK OF ASKING MUCH FROM GOD

I regularly hear people discussing what the most important thing was that they learned from their theological education. It may be a particular insight into some complex area of theology, such as the teleological argument for the existence of God, or some other aspect of doctrine. For me, the single most important aspect of my Cambridge education was learned from Dr Margaret Bowker, one of my lecturers –

but not in a classroom, rather one-to-one. She was the lady who taught me how to pray.

Dr Bowker, a much-respected academic, was not a theologian but a historian. She was married to the Dean of Trinity College, Cambridge. At one time in her life she had suffered badly with a form of cancer and during that time she made a deal with God. She promised the Lord that if she was healed and restored she would dedicate her life to teaching others how to pray. I was one of the people who benefited from that deal.

Over many months I learned so much from Margaret, but one thing that stood out for me was the fact that she would always want to know what I had asked for in prayer and whether I'd received what I'd asked for. Fundamental to her prayer life was the belief that every day our prayers had to ask something of God. Ever since then I have always asked God for specific things when I pray.

This is also a risk. People worry about asking God for things in case it is not His will or in case, seemingly, the prayer goes unanswered. (I know that my prayers are always answered, even if it is not the answer I want.) Yes, prayer is a risk, but the greater risk is that of not asking at all.

There are times when I am acutely aware that what I am asking for is very big, but can anything we ask for be bigger than God Himself? Of course not. The fact is, the more seemingly impossible the thing we are asking for, the greater the opportunity for God to display His goodness and glory.

I am constantly faced with asking "big" owing to the nature of our ministry. It is not unusual for me to say to the Lord, "Father, I need $150,000 in the next three days." Naturally speaking, I cannot think how such a request can be answered, but God knows! More to the point, where there exists a need among His children, He always answers such prayers. We must be willing to ask much of God and not be afraid. He is not offended by the earnest requests of His children.

The risk of seeking reconciliation

My life of working for reconciliation has been one full of risk. It is a major risk to bring together people from opposite sides of a hostile debate in the hope of finding at least a tiny bit of common ground on which they can begin a dialogue. Bringing together Muslims and Christians, Israelis and Palestinians, Shia and Sunni – all such occasions carry huge risk as one side confronts those they consider "the others" – those whom they have hated, even wanted to wipe out. The first step in reconciliation is therefore making an attempt to know and love our enemies.

Nearly all the Iraqi leaders I have worked with have hated Israelis – not just the Muslims, but the Christians too. When I began working there, it soon came to my notice that, in Iraq, no religious leader would contemplate meeting with an Israeli and none of them had ever met a Jewish rabbi. So I had a fairly simple, but radical, idea about bringing Iraqi and Israeli religious leaders together. Never before had such a meeting taken place.

I began asking senior Iraqi leaders if they would be prepared to meet the Israelis. Most were not. I asked if they would be willing to meet some Israeli Arabs. They were sceptical about that – most had little concept that there was anyone other than Jews living in Israel. Then I approached Israeli and Palestinian leaders to see what their reaction was. Their perception was that the Iraqi Shias had close links with Israel's enemy, Iran, and at first they could not believe they were being asked to meet Iraqis. For their part, the Palestinians had no problem dialoguing with Israeli Jews, but similarly hated Shia Muslims, since their Muslims were all Sunni.

I spent a long time trying to persuade the Sunni leaders that the Shia could be their friends and not their enemies. I explained that my heart was to work towards peace for our broken land. I also explained how the leaders involved in the Alexandria Declaration, although from opposing sides, had actually become friends through the process. If Jews and Palestinians could become friends, then there was hope for Sunnis and Shias, who were both Muslim.

Eventually, leaders on all sides were persuaded that it was a good idea to meet and plans could begin to arrange a suitable venue. It was not going to be easy to find somewhere appropriate. The Iraqis could not travel to Israel and the Israelis could not visit most Muslim nations. It was decided that Cyprus could be a suitable neutral venue, and so we arranged to hold the meeting in Paphos in the south-west.

Paphos was part of the Anglican Diocese of Cyprus and the Gulf, of which we in Iraq were a part. This meant we immediately had the support of a large number of churches on the island, both Anglican and evangelical, who were totally behind the venture. The prayer support from local Christians was truly tangible and together the churches agreed that they would provide 24/7 prayer support for the meeting.

With regard to risk, the Iraqis involved were literally taking their lives in their hands by agreeing to the meeting and would almost certainly have been killed for attending.

Their identities have been protected and their names don't appear anywhere in this book.

The meeting itself was incredible. The Iraqi delegation told me that they had come to the meeting hating the Jews and wanting them wiped off the face of the earth. "Now we have been together and looked in one another's eyes," one person said, "we love them." Similarly, the Jews said that they had lived in fear of the Shia, but that after three days together – as one person so wonderfully put it – fear had been "cancelled".

There is huge risk in reconciliation, but this is a good example of what happens when enemies come together and hear each other's stories. The same is true in our personal lives. It is so true that our enemies are often "friends whose stories we haven't heard yet".

I cannot mention the risk of reconciliation without recalling a man who has been one of my greatest heroes throughout all my years in Iraq. He is not an Iraqi or a religious leader, but a soldier, the American General David Petraeus. At one time, General Petraeus was the commanding officer of the Coalition forces in Baghdad. He took great risks and was instrumental in bringing opposing factions together to work towards peace. There are few people I've met in life whom I so admire. Despite what the press may say to the contrary, I know that he is a great child of God and I love him – not exactly what one expects to hear someone say about a general, but it's true. I often think that if he were still in Iraq, we would not be confronted with the level of crisis and tragedy we are now facing. I honour David Petraeus as a true risk-taker for reconciliation.

The risk of engaging with our enemies

Part of the risk of reconciliation work is that of dealing with bad people. I have always said that peacemaking is not about dealing with nice people. The very fact that people are caught up in conflict means that at least some of them must have been the cause of it. Those who turn to violence in order to achieve their own ends are not usually good people. Most think that their aims and ideals justify their radical actions, but to others this is terrorist activity.

Often I find myself sitting with leaders of radical groups such as Hamas or the Islamic State of Iraq (ISIS) – groups who are both involved in extreme terrorist activity – but the only way one can bring about change is by working with them. Someone has to risk loving them so that change might be possible, from the inside out. Change can happen, but it takes time and requires perseverance.

This type of work does put me at risk. The very fact of meeting the leaders of such organizations, getting to know who they are and where to find them, means one has vital intelligence – and there are other people who want that intelligence. If such intelligence can be obtained about one's enemies, then it is possible to hunt them down and take them out. And what about the person who possesses that intelligence? The fact is, if you don't share it, then the lives of people close to you may be threatened. This is the kind of ethical dilemma I am constantly faced with in Iraq.

At least when one brings enemies together there is the hope that something can be done to reduce violence and help bring about peace. The very act of being willing to sit down and begin a dialogue, however tense it may be, is the first sign of hope for reconciliation. In such situations it is not my job to judge who is right and who is wrong, but to facilitate an honest, open dialogue, getting each side to listen to the other side's story.

Before our major meeting of religious leaders in 2002 we met in a secret location in Jerusalem. Often we would meet late at night and talk into the early hours of the morning. Slowly, week after week, sworn enemies heard each other's stories and began to see that they all had at least two things in common: firstly, they were all minorities, and, secondly, they had all suffered grave loss – a loss of liberty, property, territory, and, ultimately, power. Over time they found some common ground and began to appreciate each other's point of view. I witnessed enemies becoming friends.

It is interesting to see how people respond to friends who used to be their enemies. During the time when I brought the Israeli and Palestinian leaders to London, we attended a press conference and two of the representatives stood side by side – Rabbi Michael Melchior, then foreign minister of Israel, and the late Sheikh Talal Al-Sadr, a former Palestinian Authority minister. At one point, someone heckled from the audience, shouting loudly, asking the Sheikh why he was with this "evil Zionist leader". Sheikh Talal took Rabbi Melchior's hand and said, "Rabbi Melchior is my brother. We will walk the long and difficult road to reconciliation together."

THE RISK OF TRUSTING GOD TO KEEP US SAFE

I have heard it said that the essence of our walk with God is overcoming our "trust issues" with Him: trusting that He really will provide for us as He says; trusting that He really will protect us from danger if we take a risk on His behalf.

The majority of my life is lived in Baghdad, which is a very dangerous place. As I write, there have been three recent suicide bombings within walking distance of the church where I live and work. A number of people have been shot and killed today. One of them was the person who was supposed to drive me to the US Embassy. Each day, I cannot know the risks that will have to be faced or what tragedies may occur.

This is my "norm". I appreciate that it is not normal for most people, but we can all relate to needing to trust our heavenly Father more – to becoming completely dependent on Him. We tend to cling on to things in our lives and we fear letting go, but it is only as we admit our need and vulnerability that the Lord can take control and protect and care for us.

I have never once worried about being in Iraq, because I know that God has called me to be here – and when God calls us to be somewhere, we can be sure that He will provide for us. Don't take care; take risks. Nothing worthwhile was ever achieved that didn't involve an element of risk.

CHAPTER 19

A Normal Day

People often ask me to describe a "typical day" in my life. In truth, no day is very typical, but in this chapter and the next I will try to provide small and large snapshots of my life.

I wake up at 5.30 a.m. Today is Monday, so a normal day without services. I start the day with prayer and Bible reading. I always begin by asking the Lord what passage he would like me to speak on when I next preach and then, according to His answer, I read that passage and pray around it. I am due to speak at some GOD TV revival meetings this coming weekend. Romans 8:17–18 is coming to me loud and clear:

> Now if we are children, then we are heirs – heirs of God and co-heirs with Christ, if indeed we share in his sufferings in order that we may also share in his glory. I consider that our present sufferings are not worth comparing with the glory that will be revealed in us. (NIV)

God's answer has to be loud and clear because He knows I do not really want to speak on these verses. I've done so many times before and I find it difficult. Nevertheless, God has asked me to speak about suffering again, so I'll obey Him.

By 7.15 a.m. I have finished my prayers and reading for the day and it takes me about half an hour to get out of bed. I should mention that my one room in St George's is a multifunctional space. It is my office, study, meeting room, dining room, and bedroom! At 7.45 a.m. Dina, our housekeeper, brings me a cup of tea. This is the only sustenance I'll have until after dark today because it is Ramadan and we can't actually obtain any food until after sunset. With my tea, I go to my laptop to do some writing.

Politically, the challenges for us in Iraq are very great at the moment. Despite the fact that in 2014 a new prime minister was appointed, Haider al-Abadi, his government is not in control of much of the country, as a large part of it is now in the grip of the terrorist group ISIS. Uncertainty remains and nobody knows what will happen now in Iraq. I phone a few journalist friends to see if there is anything we need to touch base on today. Then I try to phone some of the other church leaders in the area, but as usual find it virtually impossible to get through. There is a lot of fear among everyone about what is happening in Baghdad, with the very real risk of ISIS storming the city and taking control. If that danger appears to be imminent then it will be too dangerous for Christians to remain, and we will need to get them out of the country, to the north, into Kurdistan. The decision whether to stay or flee balances on a knife edge.

After making these calls I venture out to visit our school and clinic. The school has over 100 children from kindergarten age up to seven. Our clinic has a variety of medical specialists, general practitioners and dentists, as well as laboratory and pharmacy staff. I chat to all the staff and encourage them and thank them for their service. We give thanks to God that we are able to provide all of our treatment free to many needy people.

After this it is time to go out of our complex and pay a quick visit to one of my favourite places – the Home for Disabled Children. I have visited here regularly ever since my first trip to Iraq sixteen years ago. The home has existed for twenty years, set up by Mother Teresa to care for the disabled and abandoned children of Iraq, most of whom have severe deformities. The sisters who run the home are all from India and visiting them is always a cause for great joy. They speak English with wonderful Indian accents. We are very close to one another, like family, and I always aim to provide something nice for the children each time I visit.

After this, I return to my church HQ and Dr Sarah and Sally Multi arrive (I will speak more about them in a later chapter). Together we talk through the plans for the remainder of the day. Top of our list for action is my need to meet with a top Sunni sheikh. He is one of the most senior Sunnis involved in the fragmented Iraqi government. We phone his team and they agree to arrange a meeting for later in the day.

Now it is mid-morning and, as is normal, people begin arriving and asking to see me. They have various problems and requests for help. We promise to help those with medical problems through our clinic. Several people need particular medication, so I send them to our pharmacy. By 1.00 p.m. I have seen around half a dozen people, some of whom also needed financial help. We gave them as much as we could.

During the afternoon I take a call from my office in the UK. Someone wants me to contact an Iraqi Christian they met while on holiday in Turkey. I manage to track him down, make contact, and arrange to meet up with him. I invite him to come and worship with us. I put the phone down from this very positive conversation and immediately a huge boom shakes the building. There has been another explosion. It will have been another suicide bomber or a nearby car bomb.

At some point each day I will call to speak to my colleagues at the US Embassy. It is usually to receive a breakdown of the latest intelligence in the area, though this is becoming increasingly difficult as many people have left the Embassy because of the danger. I chat to the one person I'm able to get hold of, but in reality they are more interested in the intelligence I can give them than vice versa. After all, they are cocooned in their vast razor-wired fortress and I am outside. I describe what is going on and repeat what we've heard people saying on the ground.

In general, things are not looking good. The Embassy fears the breaking out of full-blown war in a matter of days. They are worried about my being stuck out in the Red Zone (the real Baghdad). I tell them I'll be leaving for England tomorrow, which reassures them. I don't tell them that I have every intention of returning in a few days.

This conversation suddenly reminds me – I am returning to England tomorrow and need to prepare! I will be travelling to Plymouth to speak at the GOD TV event there. I will also fit in a meeting with my old friend Justin Welby, the Archbishop of Canterbury. All of this means I need to run a quick errand – to the nearby Abu Afif's Chocolate Shop. It is totally bizarre that in the midst of the trauma of Baghdad you can find the most exquisite, luxurious chocolate you'll find anywhere in the world. Before I go back to England, I always pay a quick visit here to stock up. I can show people that there is at least one good thing in Baghdad!

After this I have a scheduled meeting with my curate, Faiz. He is the only Iraqi who has been ordained as an Anglican priest. We sit down and talk in depth about the major problems that we face. The extreme terrorist group ISIS, now simply called Islamic State, has taken over much of Iraq, setting up bases in Mosul and Nineveh. The traditional home of many of the Christians has been taken over by these Sunni terrorists. Over a million people have moved out of Mosul. We talk about the reality of what we as a church now face. ISIS say they will take Baghdad, and they are now only twenty miles away. The government assure us that they will prevent them from entering Baghdad, but after seeing the last encounter between ISIS and the Iraqi army we are not totally convinced.

We talk about what we should do. It is clear that we remain in great danger if we stay. We may perhaps have to move to Erbil – many of our people have already gone there and so there is a congregation waiting for us. What we do not have is any kind of base there – a church or a place to live. We discuss the painful possibility of having to leave our church complex, our clinic, our school. We pray and thank God that, despite this terrible crisis, we have had sufficient funds donated to cope with the tremendous needs that confront us.

After this, more visitors come to see me. A couple arrive, bringing their son to be prayed for. He is in his late teens and is totally unable to hear. As a result he has never been to school and is very depressed. I hug him to show him that I love him, and then I pray for him and anoint him with oil. I give him a cross and one of my books that has lots of pictures in it. Then I talk with his parents about other needs that the family have and I promise to help them regularly if I can.

By now sunset is fast approaching and I have eaten nothing all day. Dr Sarah, our Iraqi director, is my main assistant as well as being one of our dental surgeons. She goes off to get us some food and returns in due course with a kebab for me. Sally Multi joins us, as do two other honorary members of our family, Rita (ten) and George (eight). We sit, surrounded by food, and talk.

While finishing my kebab, by telephone I join in a meeting of my Foundation's US board. Most of the board have previously served in Baghdad; it is made up of individuals ranging from former military men to high-level diplomats. Among them is Ambassador Paul Bremer, one-time leader of the Coalition Provisional Authority. Our Executive Director is retired Brigadier General David Greer, also a member of my US Embassy congregation in Baghdad. I officiated at David's wedding to Susan, a wonderful lady who was also a member of our Embassy congregation. Not many Westerners can say they were married in Iraq's Green Zone against a backdrop of rocket fire. At least it was a truly memorable occasion.

Though it is after dark, my day is nowhere near finished yet. I still have the Sunni Sheikh to go and see. I am driven over to meet him and the meeting is short and to the point. Together we have a major meeting to plan. We discuss what is happening with the Iraqi government and also ISIS. I mention the fact that I have discovered that one of my friends, a Sunni tribal leader, has in fact joined Daash,[10] the Sunni terrorist group.

---

10 The name "Daash" is an acronym for "Dulat al-Islam fi al-Iraq wal-Sham" – "the Islamic State in Iraq and Greater Syria", and it is a Sunni Salafi organization.

When I arrive back at the church and enter my room I return to writing about current events. It is now 11.30 p.m. Shortly I will have my evening prayers and then retire. It is the end of a fairly normal eighteen-hour day.

The next day I mention to Dr Sarah that yesterday I worked for eighteen hours. She assures me that I regularly do this, and more. I do. It is the reality of my calling and this life of service.

CHAPTER 20

The Bigger Picture

My "normal" day gives a good insight into my daily life, but an overview of the events of a couple of weeks helps explain the bigger picture.

As I write, I am on a plane from London to Israel, having completed my weekend speaking engagement for GOD TV. On this trip I once again had the help of my friend Terry Jones, a retired police officer whom I got to know during my time in Coventry. Terry is a dynamic guy who is able to make things happen, and so is the perfect companion for me. He is always there for me when I need him.

On this trip I also met my old friend and colleague Justin Welby. Seeing him is always such a pleasure. We had a comprehensive talk about major issues concerning Israel and Palestine, and then discussed the matters affecting the Christians in Mosul and Nineveh who have been forced out of their homes and churches.

I arrive in Israel at a time of all-out war between Israel and Gaza. Hamas militants in Gaza have been continually shelling Israel and Israel has responded with fierce attacks. Everyone is frightened on both sides. Everyone feels marginalized by the media. Each side is convinced that they are the ones who are in the right. Once again, the story of my life is repeating itself. My task is to try to show both sides the pain that the other is suffering and work with them to seek peace.

I stay in the Jerusalem Hills Inn, run by my great friends Chaim and Ruti Singerman, which is located in the Arab town of Abu Ghosh on the outskirts of Jerusalem. They have seven wonderful children. I confess that two of their children are very special to me. First there is Sarah, their eldest daughter, who is nineteen and currently completing her military service, working in communications. She is a wonderful worship leader and, when she sings, the presence of God comes.

Then there is Josiah, aged ten, also known as Yoshi, just like my oldest son. When I see him I give him a big hug and he holds on tight to me. Like my Yoshi back in England he has the most amazing grasp of politics, and we talk about the most difficult issues. Today we chat about the political situation in the Middle East and Yoshi has very clear ideas on what the regional political leaders should do. The following day I will see former government minister Rabbi Michael Melchior and he will say, almost word for word, what Yoshi has said.

A few months earlier Ruti gave birth to another baby girl, called Sheri. Yoshi is upset because now there are more girls than boys in the family. I chat to him and wonder what we can do to rectify this situation. It so happens that I have some honorary adopted children in Iraq. One of them, Amar, is a boy the same age as Yoshi, and Amar is an only child – he has always wanted a brother. I suggest that Yoshi and Amar become "brothers" and in due course they do! Now, every time I visit Israel I set up a phone call so that they can chat with each other. It is not possible to telephone Israel from Iraq, but we can do it this way round.

After staying with the Singermans I move into Jerusalem and stay at Christ Church in the Old City, which houses the Israeli headquarters of the Church's Ministry among Jewish People, of which I am Vice-President. I love meeting with David Pillegi, the rector, and the church is centrally located, so perfect for getting to a wide variety of meetings. I am not very good at keeping secrets, but much of my work in this area is confidential, so I can't write about it.

I have one meeting that I can mention, with the foreign minister. We discuss the Israel–Gaza crisis and how to deal with it. I make it clear that there are significant things we *could* do but are prevented from doing by the fact that no Israelis are allowed into Gaza at present. Despite this difficulty we will keep doing what we can to achieve peace. I also speak with the minister about the rise of Arab militants in the region and their threat to Israel. It is a grave threat and it is not clear how this situation will play out.

From Israel I fly back to England for several more speaking events. First I go to speak at my old parish church in Clapham. I have been invited back because they have just heard about my winning this year's Wilberforce Award. It is wonderful to visit there and meet so many of my old congregation.

I spend the night in London with my colleagues before going to preach at Chiswick Christian Centre the next morning. I love this church – a lovely group of people to worship and spend time with. Then, in the evening, I speak at another great church in Guildford, the town where Josiah attended school. Present is one of his former teachers.

Before I return to Iraq my main office is contacted by the office of HRH Prince Charles. The Prince's private secretary would like to meet me. It is so encouraging to realize that we are not forgotten here in Iraq.

The next day I begin the journey back to Iraq via Jordan. When I finally arrive in Baghdad I am greeted by my security team. After travelling around the south of England suddenly I am confronted with the harsh reality of Iraq. As I travel back to St George's my armoured vehicle is surrounded by a large number of similar trucks full of armed soldiers whose weapons are pointing in every direction. The size of this moving shield and the amount of firepower seem utterly disproportionate, but the security risk in Baghdad is the greatest I have ever experienced.

People here are gripped with fear about what is happening with ISIS. Many of the people I meet have relatives in Mosul or Nineveh. ISIS have not yet entered Baghdad, but there have been random attacks on people and an increase in the number of kidnappings. People continue to flee the area in their masses, but the sad fact is, things remain dire even for those who have left. Most have gone to Turkey, but they have been told it will take several years to obtain an interview with the UNHCR to see whether they are eligible to be resettled as refugees. Until then they will live in awful limbo.

We continue to hope in the Lord despite the fierce sectarian division that exists. We may be attacked from outside by Sunni terrorists, but here the Sunnis are already being attacked by Shia militia. Today several Sunnis were killed and their bodies hung up in the street on public display. This is the reality of how bad things are. I always used to say to our congregation, "Don't you leave me, because I'm not leaving you." Now all I can say is, "I'm not leaving you." How can I expect our congregation to stay when things are so awful?

After this dreadful news, the next day I receive some joyous news. Dawood, my adopted son, and his wife, Sandy, have had a baby boy. Dawood and Sandy fled the country to go to Canada. Their baby will be called "Andrew Dawood Andrew". According to Iraqi tradition, the child's chosen name is followed first by his father's name and then by his grandfather's name – hence my name appears twice. I miss them all so much and wish they could be here with me, but, of course, it is not safe. Dawood had to flee the country when spies discovered he was planning a meeting for me between Iraqi and Israeli leaders. As a result, his life was in danger.

Later I receive a visit from our Archdeacon, the Venerable Bill Schwartz, who oversees the Anglican Church in the entire Gulf region, which includes Iraq and Yemen. There is much we need to discuss, not least the long-term future of the church. In truth, we don't know what the long-term prospects are. We don't know what will be happening in one month's time, let alone a year or more. Will there even be an Iraq as we know it? One thing is certain: it will be a very different Iraq from what it is now.

The next major event in my diary is a trip to Israel to participate in a GOD TV programme on the Middle East, broadcast from Jerusalem. Most of the interview is about the immense suffering that our people are going through. So much of my life is spent dealing with journalists, being interviewed, going to radio/TV studios, or being followed by a camera crew. To be honest, there are days when I wish I'd never have to do another interview again, but life doesn't really work like that. Our people often tell me that they feel forgotten. The most horrendous crimes in recent history are happening in our midst and the story is not being told. This is why I continue to do interviews and write books – so that the story may be heard.

There are some in the media, however, who are committed to getting our story told. A short while ago, Jane Arraf, a well-known journalist who has worked with CNN and is now with Al Jazeera, arrived with a team to cover what is happening to us in Iraq. They were with us for a long weekend – Friday to Monday – and filmed everything they could, apart from our service in the US Embassy, which was, of course, off limits. In due course her programme will be aired in the US on the PBS channel.

The Friday-evening youth meeting was as good as ever, with great worship and praise in the midst of our adversity. There was obvious fear among our young people, but worshipping together gives them hope. Jane enjoyed being with our youth and was struck by the light that exists in the midst of such darkness. Afterwards, as is our custom, we all had dinner together.

The next day is Saturday and we have our service at the Embassy. A much smaller group of people attend because all non-essential staff have been removed from the Embassy owing to the onslaught of ISIS. Nevertheless, we have a good service in this little space, cocooned inside the real world outside. There is still a strong sense that these people are "our people" and the love shared between us is tangible.

I return to our compound for a continuous stream of phone interviews with different radio and TV stations. In the evening the BBC decide they want me for a live TV interview. We are only one mile away from the studio that will host this, but getting there is a nightmare as we need to pass through endless security checkpoints. It takes over an hour to travel the one mile and the interview is short, but it will be broadcast on the BBC World News, so I know that the message will travel around the world.

The following morning is Sunday and this usually begins with my speaking live on several Christian radio programmes based in England. When there is a crisis it's not unusual for me to have spoken with ten different stations before going to conduct our church service. Today, however, I am scheduled to do an interview with Fox News and they have insisted it must be live, so I am up at 2.00 a.m. this Sunday morning to speak to them via Skype. After speaking to someone I am effectively put on hold for a whole hour, since news has broken of a famous actor dying. I am still waiting at 3.30 a.m., when I give up. Once again I find the media frustrating, but Dr Sarah reminds me that there is no one else to tell our story.

The crisis in Iraq continues to get worse, and though we plan as best we can, often our plans turn out to be futile. Erbil is no longer the safe haven it was and access to it has been banned. Thousands of Christians and other minorities have taken refuge there. We have been feeding thousands of people in the area and supporting various Christian leaders who, in turn, are trying to support their people. So our main work has become supporting those who have fled the evil actions of ISIS, who are still causing havoc in Iraq but have not yet got into Baghdad.

At the moment our work here is very intensive. I have just been informed that some terrorists have kidnapped a number of Christian girls and have put them up "for sale". We are seeing if it is possible for us to buy them back. What a horrendous situation. This is the nature of the crisis we are in. What can we do? In all things we continue to pray and ask God for His help and, somehow, His supernatural presence continues to sustain us.

CHAPTER 21

My Choice

People often ask me why I choose to live my life in the way that I do. First of all, I have to acknowledge that I did indeed choose it. No one forced me to do what I do, or to live and work in one of the most dangerous places in the world. God called me to do it and yet He never forced me to go. He never violates His children's free will. I still had a choice. I chose to follow where He led me.

But I do love my life. I appreciate that most people could not live the way I do, but since my youth I have always loved adventure, excitement, and risk taking. It takes a certain type of person to be a member of a hospital crash team, just as it takes a certain type of person to live in a war zone. I have never wanted a quiet life. I have never wanted to conform to the norm.

Nothing was more exciting for me than to step in and help save the life of a patient with a ruptured aortic aneurism – a life-or-death situation in which one has to respond radically and quickly. Years later, as a priest, I had no desire to settle down in a nice, suburban parish, drinking tea and eating cucumber sandwiches! I feel more at home in an active war zone, where danger and crises go with the territory.

That is not to say that I like what is happening around me. I don't like the fact that Baghdad is caught up in a war, just as I didn't like it when major medical emergencies occurred at St Thomas' Hospital. But the fact is, I like to respond to a crisis. When God calls us to something, He always provides us with the skills and wisdom we need to get the job done. He made me to thrive in an emergency.

Not only does God give us the skills we need, He also gives us joy in the performance of our ministry. People find it difficult to understand how I can be joyful in the midst of such dire, tragic circumstances in Iraq, and when I go to speak at a church the people are nearly always surprised that I am a joyful person, not grim-faced and sombre. As I go about my daily work in Baghdad I am very rarely sad; I am mostly joyful. When you feel as though you are doing what you're called to do in life, and therefore have the best job in the world, surely that is a reason to be happy.

Naturally, I am very sad when people I know and love in Iraq are killed, but one lesson I have learned through this ministry is that when I am knocked down I must get back up again. I don't get knocked down very often, but when I do, I make sure that I get up and carry on quickly. Why? Because there are still so many people in need and no one else is going to help them.

SUSTAINED BY LOVE

Despite the difficulties of this job and the constant danger that I face, I am overwhelmed by the continual love and support of others. God's love surrounds me and I am so aware of His manifest presence. His love is also demonstrated through the love of so many others. When I think about how many people express their love and care for me, it is so immense that I find it deeply humbling and often ask myself, "Why?" I recall days or years gone by when I didn't seem to have any real friends, and now I have so many.

As I write this chapter I am at home in the UK, ill with hepatitis. I remember from my medical days how we all lived in fear of this illness. I have to accept the fact that I probably contracted it because of the terrible hygiene of my living conditions in Baghdad. I knew that I might be attacked physically, kidnapped and tortured, or blown up, but the fact that I might get a serious infectious illness never occurred to me. It is at difficult times like this that one has to put into practice the reality of living in hope. As the words of Edward Mote's 1834 hymn say, "My hope is built on nothing less than Jesus' blood and righteousness."

As I look back over all that God has done in my life so far, I am amazed by how His plan and purpose for me has unfolded. I had an inkling of my destiny as a small boy, and I can only do what I do now because of the journey on which God has led me. The most thrilling aspect of this to me is the fact that no part of my training has been left behind. Nothing God led me to do has been wasted.

Who would ever have thought that a priest with a medical background would be running a church in a war zone with its own clinic, treating over 150 patients each day? I still think it is strange that the doctors come to me for assistance when they are having difficulty putting in intravenous lines – there aren't too many priests who can assist with that!

Then there is our pioneering stem-cell treatment. People travel to us from all over the world to be treated and, as I mentioned earlier, it has been vital in treating my MS. So our little church in the midst of tragedy and devastation has become an oasis of healing.

I could never have guessed that God's training and equipping would lead me to be involved in all of this, in an increasingly radical Shia Islamic state in the Middle East. Yet, as I survey the situation around me, there is nowhere I would rather be. I see it all as the work of the Almighty.

HE IS EXTRAORDINARY; I AM NOT

This morning, despite being unwell at the moment, I spoke on a London radio station. They introduced me in quite a bizarre way, calling me a "bold, heroic individual". I was there to speak about the really important subject of the terrorist activity of the Islamic State, but instead I spent the first two minutes explaining why I am not a hero. I don't think I won the argument, but I tried.

I find it difficult when people treat me as some kind of great or mystical figure. This week alone has provided two examples. The first was the aforementioned radio presenter; then the next day I was contacted by a senior member of the Conservative Party, who wanted to know if I was prepared to stand for the position of Mayor of London. He told me that they needed a dynamic, charismatic individual and that I met all the requirements. I simply said, sorry, that is not my desire or my calling. Such flattery led to a split second of temptation, but then I thought of the apostle Peter and of how, having been called from the commercial fishing business to be a fisher of men, he could never return to his former work. I was reminded once again that my calling is to the Middle East. I cannot leave until the Lord tells me to.

My "thorn"

My health has been and continues to be a major challenge in my life. As is evident in my story, I have always had serious health problems. Yet, even now, I do not think of myself as being "ill" – it is just something that I've had to learn to live with. It is another source of humility for me, that I need to rely on the help of others to do certain basic things that other people take for granted – and that this help is given with such love and care.

I always need to have someone travelling with me to help me, for instance, owing to my limited mobility. Something as simple as carrying a cup of tea from one room to the next is impossible for me without an accident. My balance is so bad that I cannot bend down to pick up something from the floor. I can sit in a room and negotiate with world leaders, but I can't tie my own shoelaces.

Whenever I am on the BBC they make a point of telling their listeners when they introduce me that I have MS, because it affects my voice. I find this difficult to hear – it's not easy for me to accept that my diction is often flawed. But Caroline assures me that it is a good thing, because in the past people have written or phoned in to complain about the "drunk vicar" they heard on the radio!

Something else that has bothered me in recent times is the fact that I have had to sit down while preaching. I don't like doing this and there are some times, such as when lecturing at Cambridge, for instance, when I just refuse to do so, and continue to stand despite its making me feel very ill. Instead of giving in to illness, I choose to pray that God will help me to function as I should.

For me, the thorn in the flesh of Paul seems an obvious comparison. Our Lord allowed one of the greatest preachers, teachers, and pastors of all time to put up with a certain degree of suffering throughout his entire ministry, though we are not told exactly what it was. Why was this? We are given no explanation, but it gives me hope: one does not have to be in perfect shape to be a minister of the gospel. As the saying goes, God uses flawed, frail human beings to do His work, because they are the only type of humans available.

There is a claim from some sections of the church (often referred to as "the prosperity gospel") that doing God's will and following Jesus will be rewarded by good health and wealth. My personal experience doesn't include either of those, yet I can testify to the faithfulness of God in keeping His promises. I have never been wealthy, but God has always provided for all my needs and I have never gone without. God has also provided for the needs of many poor people through me, and in ways that, naturally speaking, seemed impossible.

At the heart of every ministry is the principle of servanthood. We are called to be God's servants in every aspect of life and ministry. It doesn't matter to me whether I am dealing with the poor people of Baghdad, diplomats, or heads of state – to me it is all the work of Jesus. So whether I find myself in the West or the Middle East, I seek to reflect the likeness of Jesus to everyone I meet. What greater calling can there be?

CHAPTER 22

Very Special People

In the previous chapter I spoke about being sustained by the love of God and God's love expressed through others. The Lord has been incredibly gracious to me in surrounding me with some utterly amazing people. I want to pay tribute to them in this chapter.

MY CHILDREN

I began this book by talking about the dream I had as a young boy – to be an anaesthetist and a priest. I was told that doing both was impossible, but with God all things are possible, and the course of my life was set before I was ten years old. Then I had other dreams that God has miraculously answered...

I dreamed of having a beautiful, clever wife, and God graciously gave me Caroline. Then I dreamed of having children and I have been blessed beyond measure with my two boys, Jacob and Josiah. I hoped and prayed that they would both be brilliant – and they are.

Everything was perfect, but if there was one more thing I could have wished for, it was a daughter. In due course,

God would bless me with more children – adopted ones – including some daughters!

At St George's there are many children who refer to me as "Daddy" – an affectionate term of respect. But I came to have a special connection with four children: Dawood, Lina, Fulla, and Amar. Sadly, I am not allowed to write about Lina here, owing to family circumstances, but I will speak about the others.

Dawood's story is the easiest to remember and explain. I found him living in the back of a US army tank following the Iraq war in 2003. He was twelve years old and had no one to look after him. I took him home with me and he learned to speak English in just three weeks. As he grew into a young man, he never left my side until he was forced to flee the country a short time ago. Like all boys, Dawood has had his good and bad moments, but he has been unswervingly loyal and has literally saved my life on more than one occasion.

In Iraqi Christian culture there is a particular method by which one gets married. They have no concept of a boy and girl going out, or "courting", to use the old-fashioned term; one just gets engaged and then the relationship begins. It is traditional for a child to present their intended to their parents, to receive their blessing for getting engaged. When he was of an appropriate age, Dawood would regularly bring me girls that he said he wanted to marry, but I could tell that they were not suitable for one reason or another. In all, Dawood brought thirteen girls to see me and I said no thirteen times in not very subtle ways! Then one day he turned up with a fourteenth.

This girl, Sandy, was different. I could tell that she was a godly woman who loved Jesus and instantly I knew she was perfect for Dawood. I gave them my blessing inside two minutes.

We had a wonderful engagement party for Dawood and Sandy. In Iraq, this event is almost on the same scale as a wedding. It is here that the rings are blessed and exchanged. Then we set about planning the wedding. Dawood reminded me that he'd always said he would get married on my birthday, and that is what happened. When the day came, and we were all at the wedding, Dawood brought out a huge birthday cake for me, which was wonderful and very moving.

In due course, Sandy began working for me and I came to love her like one of my own children – so God gave me a daughter. We were family together and it was one of the happiest times of my life. Dawood occasionally complains to me that I love Sandy more than him! I love them both, of course.

Fulla is not an officially adopted child, but several families asked me if I would take on looking after their children when they felt they could not, and this is what I do with Fulla. She was with me in Iraq until she moved to the US, where I still care for her financially, paying her college fees and for healthcare. Although I miss having her with me in Baghdad, she has become my unofficial assistant whenever I travel to America – which means that I still see her quite often. She also comes to visit me in Baghdad and holds the honour of being probably the only person in the world who goes to Iraq on holiday! But Iraq is her home and, if it were safe to do so, she would return to be with her people.

Then there is Amar, who is several years younger than all my other children. I met him when one of the ladies in our church came to ask me to baptize her son. It was known that one of Saddam Hussein's ministers had forced her into a marriage and Amar was the result of that marriage. The father disappeared after the war, but this lady brought her son up as a Christian and longed for him to be baptized one day. It was too great a risk to baptize anyone in public, so I took Amar into the Green Zone to do it.

It was a wonderful, emotional little service, after which Amar threw his arms around me, held me very tight, and said to me, "*Abouna*, will you be my daddy now?" (*Abouna* means "father" and is used to address a priest.) I assured Amar that I would be his daddy, and so I got a new adopted son. Even though I am no longer in Iraq, Amar and I speak regularly by phone and I love him and provide for all his needs from a distance.

All my children are the inspiration of my life and give me so much joy and a reason to persevere with the mission God has given me. They have all spent time with one another on various occasions and have no doubt that they are all brothers and sisters.

Back in England, Josiah is a quiet, studious person, whereas Jacob is loud, outrageous, and more like me! As I wrote this it was approaching Christmas, and I was thinking about presents. Jacob is easy to buy for, because he wants anything and everything. It is more difficult to buy something for Josiah. Eventually Josiah told me that he would really like me to buy him some points for a credit union account, to pay for short-term loans for people in the developing world. It is something I would never have thought of, and I think it is truly wonderful that he has a heart for others in far-flung corners of the world. Both my boys make me immensely proud to be their father.

MORE SPECIAL PEOPLE

I got to know Sally Multi when I met her family, who live in a
very poor area of the city called Baghdad al-Jadida, or "New
Baghdad". It is essentially a slum. I loved visiting there and
often saw this family and the delightful Sally. We became
very close and that is why I refer to her as Sally Multi (which
means "my Sally"). Sally left school at seventeen and came
to work for me at the church. Although I haven't officially
adopted her, she too is like a daughter to me.

DR SARAH

There are many special people who, over the years, have
made it possible for me to live my life as I do, but one of
the closest and most vital members of my team is Dr Sarah
Ahmed, my Director of Operations. This is how we met:

Every two years the Tanenbaum Center for Interreligious
Understanding has a conference that brings together all the
people who have been awarded its Peace Makers in Action
award, of which I am one. I consider it a great honour to
be a member of this incredible fraternity. One year, while
attending the conference, I heard that another conference
was taking place in the same convention centre – to bring
together young Jews and Muslims.

One day the delegates from each conference were mixing
and chatting and someone drew it to my attention that one
of the young Muslim participants in the other conference
was an Iraqi. I found it difficult to believe that any Iraqi
would choose to attend a conference with Jewish people,
knowing the extent of the Iraqis' dislike of the Jews, so I
asked to be introduced to her. In due course I met Sarah

and we began talking. I soon realized that here was a quite amazing person.

I discovered that Sarah was an Iraqi dentist who was passionate about peacemaking. I listened to what she had to say and, as she was still talking, God spoke clearly to me about her: "Take her to work with you." I recall thinking, "Lord, she's a Muslim; how can she come to work with me?" But then I thought, "Who am I to argue with God?" So I told Sarah that I had a church, a clinic, two dental surgeries, and a major ministry that was working towards reconciliation in Baghdad. I followed that up by saying, "I want you to come and work for me."

Sarah certainly didn't jump at the opportunity. Instead, she told me that she didn't want to come and work with me! She later told me that, following our chat, she went away to do some research on the Internet to find out exactly who this strange man was. I thought that was that, but a short while later she got in touch with me to say that she would come and work with me on a short-term trial basis.

So eventually Sarah arrived and we began working together. She divided her time between the dental clinic and my office. At the time I'd just lost some key office staff, so after a few days I asked her if she would consider becoming my personal assistant. She agreed, and it was not long before I discovered my life had changed for the better. Sarah transformed my working environment and I realized that here was someone who could be a real partner in every aspect of my work.

In the clinic she established herself as one of the most sophisticated and talented dentists. If there was a difficult case, it would be Sarah who was asked to deal with it. Within a short while, the patients were saying that they only wanted to see Dr Sarah.

The dental clinic was not the only place where she earned rapid respect. Although the Christian community knew that she was a Muslim, the parish quickly embraced her. She became my translator at our midweek services and events. She had the greatest impact in our Friday-night youth meeting, because not only is she an outstanding interpreter, but she also has a vibrant, engaging personality and the young people love her.

Sarah has since become deeply involved in the comprehensive relief work of the church, as we seek to meet a wide variety of needs in the community. On one occasion I took her with me into Baghdad al-Jadida, which was an unusual event in itself, since upper-middle-class Iraqis never venture into the slum area of the city and Sarah had never set foot there. While there, I thought it strange that there were sheep wandering around the streets, since there is not a blade of grass to be seen. I wondered out loud, "What on earth do these sheep eat?" and Sarah replied, "Garbage." I'm afraid she was right – I never saw them do anything other than rummage for food amid the rubbish that lies strewn across the streets.

On all of our visits, Sarah would always examine the teeth of every person in every house we visited. Iraq's standard of dental hygiene is among the worst in the world. There is no culture of visiting the dentist for a check-up – people go only when they are in agony and need a tooth removed. But, with Sarah, in addition to the food we distributed, there would also be toothbrushes and toothpaste to give out. The people thought this was wonderful.

Sarah also assists me in my reconciliation work. You may guess that it is not generally acceptable for a woman to play a role in engaging with major Islamic leaders, but Dr

Sarah is different. She is able to grasp and interpret the most complex religious discussions and communicate them in such a way as to move things forward. Nowadays, religious leaders don't ask when I am next coming to see them; they ask when Dr Sarah is coming! She continues to play a major role in our international reconciliation meetings.

Sarah is like one of my family now, and has had an impact not only on my work life but on my home life too. She rapidly developed a very close friendship with Caroline and I think it is true to say that they never disagree on anything. In fact, if Caroline ever finds it difficult to persuade me to do something, she just asks Sarah to get me to do it!

Sarah has also become great friends with Jacob and Josiah. On a recent trip to Los Angeles, she took the boys to see the LA Clippers basketball team play when I wasn't well enough to do so. They had a fantastic time and the fact is, I think that Sarah gets along with them so well because she is more than capable of joining in with their boyish pranks!

OTHER SUPPORT STAFF

Sarah is one of four people who effectively run my life. There is Caroline, of course, and then also Lesley Kent, my PA in the UK, and Terry Jones, whom I mentioned in the previous chapter, who travels with me.

Lesley is amazing. She is in her sixties, but rides a Harley Davidson motorcycle to the office and has no plans to stop doing so! Lesley works from my home office in Hampshire, UK, and manages all my speaking engagements in both the UK and overseas. She also arranges all my travel and so virtually every day speaks to a young man named Stuart at our travel agency. We constantly tease her about her relationship with Stuart! People often ask me where exactly I live and I tell them it is Seat 1D on an aeroplane, so I suppose Stuart must be my landlord!

Retired police officer Terry Jones is sixty-seven but says he is nineteen in his head, and as far as I can see this is true. Two years ago he began travelling with me to various parts of the Middle East and he is now my right-hand man. He is central to my work, as I don't know how I could function without him. What's more, he has passed the test of our ministry: he has an equal love for both Jews and Arabs. This may sound like a light thing, but it is not – so many people struggle with despising one or the other group.

I have a great team who also help to run my UK office. There is Fiona, our office manager, David, our financial manager, Daniel, our project officer, and Gehad, whom I mentioned earlier in this book, who is an Iraqi Christian and functions as our Arabic translator and IT consultant. Then there are three further part-timers, Angela, Caroline, and Michael, working in admin and finance.

Last but not least, there is Phillip, who acts as my special assistant and driver. Like Lesley, he has been with me for several years and helps me to be in the right place at the right time. The story of how I met him is rather interesting. He often used to come and babysit for the boys when they were small. One day Jacob came up to me and said that I must give Phillip a job. He was rather persistent, so I thought I should at least meet him and see what he could do, if indeed he was inclined to work with us. After a week's trial it was clear that Phillip was a multi-talented individual who fitted very well into my personal management team. So he came to work for me and, in my absence, instantly fell into the role of surrogate father to Jacob and Josiah.

* * *

I have written about my wonderful wife, Caroline, and inspirational sons, Jacob and Josiah, and mentioned my adopted children. Now, at the close of this book, I want to mention the other people whom I love so much and who are like the fire in my bones – my godchildren. There are rather a lot of them!

Leilani Locket Bliss Haney: her grandmother is an African American who worked with me in my operating-theatre days. Leilani is now also a mother of two children.

Mark and Oliver Roberts: these twin boys were born seriously premature in London and spent many days in the neonatal intensive care unit at Hammersmith Hospital, where I baptized them both.

Alexander Muir: he is the son of Maria Muir, one of my closest friends from our student days at St Thomas' Hospital. It was Maria who persuaded me to go to Cambridge and not Oxford.

Alice Cross: Alice is the daughter of friends of ours from the first parish I worked in, St Mark's, Battersea Rise, in London. Her father is an organist and played the organ at my wedding.

Sasha Watson: Sasha is the daughter of two of my former St Thomas' colleagues and I also married her parents. She too was born very prematurely and I remember the hours I spent praying by her side in the special care baby unit at the hospital.

Isaac Hart: Isaac is the son and grandson of two sets of great friends. His grandparents are Lord and Lady Reading. Lord Reading was a close colleague when he was an active member of the House of Lords. His daughter, Natasha, came to work with me for a while and married a student,

David Hart, whom I met and became friends with while in residence at Clare College, Cambridge. I eventually had the joy of officiating at their wedding.

Hannah-Rivkah: the final godchild I mention is my Hannah-Rivkah, the closest to me of all my beloved godchildren. We often discuss why we are so close and can only conclude that it must be because of God. She was born in Israel on the highway before her father was able to get her mother to hospital. I dedicated her underneath a lemon tree in the courtyard of Christ Church, Jaffa Gate, in the Old City of Jerusalem.

Sadly, her parents soon separated and her early life was very difficult, but she has a profound faith in and love for Jesus. Hannah-Rivkah went on to study Arabic at London University and is now taking a year out in Jordan – a place I pass through regularly, so we get to see each other quite frequently and we talk most days by phone. Not so long ago I was able to take her with me to Israel. It was the first time she had been there since she was a baby and we prayed together underneath the lemon tree where I dedicated her. She is another of the great gifts God has given me.

Thank you, dear reader, for indulging me as I have mentioned so many people who are special in my life. I could not have written a book about my life without mentioning them, because my life would not be what it is without them. Every day I thank God that He has been gracious enough to allow these wonderful people to make up the rich fabric of my existence. With them and our Lord, I can do everything.

Afterword: Tariq Aziz

Today should be the funeral of one of the people closest to Saddam Hussein, his deputy, Tariq Aziz. Coming from a Christian background, he was both revered and feared and yet there were many who respected him. For me it is a very personal story. At the moment the Iraqi government won't allow his body to leave Iraq for Jordan, where his family all are. We are working on it.

The fact is that if it were not for him I would not be where I am today. It was in fact he who in 1998 first got me into Iraq. Over seventeen years I would see him in so many different places. From Baghdad's Ba'ath Party offices, to grand palaces, to a prison cell in a maximum security prison.

I could write a book just on my discussions with him; indeed, I have in fact written much about him in many of my books. Every time I visited him I took him something. In all the years of our acquaintance he only ever asked for two things: first, he wanted British HP Sauce and, second, he wanted magazines and journals. You could say he wanted both the taste of freedom and the news of freedom.

I knew that, historically speaking, he was not a good man. I knew he had brought fear and death to many of the families I know and love, and yet I have to confess that I loved him. The most essential gift that the Lord has given me in my job is to be able to love my enemies, and that is what I do all the time. Enemies are not usually very nice to you. I got into the practice of inviting enemies to dinner, because I knew that enemies were people whose story you had not yet heard. The last enemy I invited to dinner – from ISIS – made it very clear that if he came he would chop my head off. So different from my experience, work, and life with Mr Aziz. The reality was that he was my friend. I will never forget two of the most important things he asked me to do. First, he wanted me to bring some of the religious leaders from Britain to Iraq and, second, he wanted me to take the religious leaders from Iraq to England and America.

Regarding England, I told him there would be no problem, The then Archbishop of Canterbury, George Carey, would help me do that, but as for America I did not know how to make it happen.

"Don't worry," he said. "Ask Billy Graham." As I have described earlier Dr Graham enlisted the help of President Bill Clinton, and the whole highly complex initiative eventually bore fruit. For me it was not only the beginning of a substantive relationship with Dr Graham but it was the beginning of an amazing relationship with the religious leaders, which has lasted to this day.

Yes, there are those who do not like my saying positive things about Tariq Aziz. I know people were very badly hurt by the Saddam regime. I know from my last meeting with him in prison that he never changed in his attitude. He made it clear to me that Iraq now was far worse than it had ever been before, and I could not disagree with him: indeed it was. Yes, I am sorry I will not see him again, and I just pray that before the end our Lord revealed Himself to him and had mercy on him.

Epilogue: Late Fragment

At the end of this book, I want to give readers an insight into the current state of our ministry in the Middle East.

PRESENT DANGER

It is a particularly difficult time as, recently, Islamic State terrorists nearly entered Baghdad. The people here are full of fear and this morning I noticed that the normally hectic local streets are deserted – no one has ventured out. News from our friends in the areas surrounding Baghdad is bleak: the terrorists are poised outside the city. No one knows precisely what is happening, but we know that civilians have been killed in air strikes and there are huge battles between ISIS and the Iraqi army.

We also know that our army is not very efficient. This morning I spoke to one of the soldiers assigned by the government to protect me. I asked him what he would do if he saw ISIS invading the city. He told me he would take off his uniform and run. I asked him if he took seriously his role as a soldier in fighting to protect his people. He replied that, no, he did not – he did it only because he needed the money.

CONCERNS FOR MY SECURITY

At 2.40 this morning I received a call from one of the security chiefs at the US Embassy. The Embassy had been contacted by a congressman from Washington, DC, Trent Franks, who was very concerned about my security. Mr Franks had, in turn, been contacted by one of our US Foundation's board members. Security is a constant topic of discussion. I am no longer allowed a badge to get into Baghdad's Green Zone. I am allowed access to the US and British Embassies, but I cannot get to them without passing through the Green Zone, so this is a constant source of frustration.

The news this morning is that the advance of ISIS towards Baghdad has been halted. Information about how far away from the city ISIS are varies depending on whom one asks, but we live in hope.

Later I went to see Frank Baker, the new British Ambassador to Iraq. To my surprise we were from exactly the same town in the UK, went to the same school, and had a lot in common. We talked at length about the situation here and about issues of security generally and my security in particular. He was happy with the security arrangements we had in place and assured me there would be additional help if I needed it.

I returned to St George's to be greeted by messages from my US board saying that they felt it was too dangerous for me to remain in Iraq and that I needed to get out quickly. They insisted that I leave immediately and travel to Israel. As I have already stated, I accept the risks as part and parcel of my ministry here, and so am naturally resistant to the idea of leaving my people.

But pressure on me to leave began to mount from a number of different sources. Among the members of the UK Foreign Office and US Congress there seemed to be equal concern. It was not long before these people were expressing their concerns in the strongest terms to the Archbishop of Canterbury. Then my own Bishop of Cyprus and the Gulf was in contact with me about his discussions with the Archbishop.

It was clear that they had decided it was now just too dangerous for me to be in Iraq – and not just in Baghdad, but also Kurdistan and other areas where I could have engaged in relief work. In the end I spoke at length to my friend Justin Welby and he told me that I was more use to my people alive than dead. I could not deny this: we were providing food, clothing, healthcare, and much more for them.

I must confess that I was so depressed by the thought of not being in Iraq that for a brief moment I considered whether I should resign from the church and continue my work here regardless, as part of a humanitarian organization. But I could not do this – I am a man under authority and I cannot just do whatever I want. It was a very hard decision to leave, but one which pleased Caroline.

Late fragment

People often ask me how they can pray for or help the believers in Baghdad. I say to them, "You can both pray for peace and pay for peace." We are extremely grateful for the prayers of other believers, but we also need practical aid to provide relief for those in dire need, so financial contributions are equally welcome.

Recently, I travelled to the US to visit a number of different places and meet some church leaders who really care about and support our mission. One of the highlights of the trip was a visit to a Christian school in Seattle. As I was being shown around, a little boy called Sean came up to me and gave me $1, telling me it was for the children in Iraq. It was a hugely moving moment and, to me, a true symbol of the widow's mite.

A few days later I was visiting the school that is based in Bethel Church, Redding, California, and I told the story of Sean's $1 gift and how I saw it as a sign of God's goodness and provision. I said that the Lord can use anyone to meet our needs and this little boy wanted to help his brothers and sisters on the other side of the world, many of whose families would have been dispersed or even killed. As I told the story, the students began to get up and come to me, each handing me their $1 or more.

For the remainder of my trip, wherever I went I told people about Sean and the response was always the same. By the end of my trip, that $1 had turned into an incredible $25,000! For me this is the perfect illustration of how God is able to take a "small" act of faith and multiply it into something amazing. That little boy had no idea of the blessing his $1 would trigger; he simply sowed a seed and left the rest in God's hands.

Back in Israel and Palestine, my story continues. My work is varied and intensive. During the last few days I have given lectures to major Israeli audiences, appeared on radio and TV, and spoken at a church in Bethlehem. Recently I became friends with a lady called Roma and her husband, Mark Burnett. I don't watch much TV, but one show I do watch with Jacob is *The Apprentice* – one of the programmes devised by Mark.[11] Mark has a heart to support the beleaguered Christians of Iraq. Before too long I will visit their home in Malibu and take Jacob with me. Suddenly I have become a hero in his eyes because I'm taking him to meet the creator of *The Apprentice*, which is far more important to me than being seen as a hero by the media!

As I look back at my journey so far, I am simply overwhelmed by the greatness and the magnificence of God in my life. I am stunned by all that He has achieved through me; amazed by how He has enabled me to survive the most horrendous situations. Above all, I am overwhelmed by God's love for me. In the end, to know the love of God and to love others truly is all we can hope for. I came across this poem by the American poet Raymond Carver called "Late Fragment".[12] I think it says everything:

And did you get what
you wanted from this life, even so?
I did.
And what did you want?
To call myself beloved, to feel myself
beloved on the earth.

This is my story so far. What will happen next, who knows? Only my Lord and my Creator: He knows!

---

11 *The Apprentice*, which began in 2005, is a British reality TV show in which a group of aspiring businessmen and -women compete for the chance to work with the business magnate Lord Alan Sugar.
12 "Late Fragment" is the final poem in Raymond Carver's (1938–1988) last published work, *A New Path to the Waterfall*, a collection written while he was dying of cancer.

THE FOUNDATION FOR RELIEF AND RECONCILIATION IN THE MIDDLE EAST

FRRME is a non-profit organization and a registered UK charity supporting the unique work of Canon Andrew White, the Emeritus Vicar of Baghdad, who led St George's Church in Baghdad until November 2014.

FRRME promotes conflict resolution in the Middle East, specialising in conflicts with a religious component to the violence. It also provides humanitarian relief and economic rejuvenation in areas where conflict has caused poverty and hardship. This work is primarily conducted in Iraq, Jordan, and Israel/Palestine.

FRRME provides vital relief – food, medicine, and shelter – to Iraqi Christian refugees who have fled the sectarian violence in Iraq.

Currently, FRRME runs a church, school, and health clinic in Amman, Jordan, where many Iraqi Christian refugees are now based. FRRME also provides relief for Iraqi Christians who are categorized as Internally Displaced People (IDP), many of whom have fled to the semi-autonomous region of Iraqi Kurdistan.

For his reconciliation work, Canon Andrew White has been awarded numerous international prizes, including the 2014 Anne Frank Special Recognition Award for Religious Tolerance and Reconciliation, as well as the 2014 William Wilberforce Award.

As part of our reconciliation work, FRRME founded the High Council of Religious Leaders in Iraq (HCRLI) which exists to bridge religious divides, enabling faith leaders to use their considerable influence to persuade people to refrain from violence, to engage politically, and to support the rule of law. It includes senior religious leaders from across Iraq's faith and ethnic groups that hold greatest political sway – Sadrists, Kurds, Sunni, Shia, and Christians.

To find out more about FRRME's work, please visit: www.frrme.org, or get in touch at: office@frrme.org